W9-DIZ-661

· THE NINE DIMENSIONS ·

MOORESVILLE PUBLIC LIBRARY
220 W. HARRISON ST.
MOORESVILLE, IN 46158
317-831-7323

· THE ·

NINE DIMENSIONS

UNVEILING THE LAWS OF ETERNITY

Ryuho Okawa

IRH PRESS

Copyright © Ryuho Okawa 2012

English Translation © Happy Science 2012

Original title: "Eien no Hō"

All rights reserved

RO Books is a registered trademark of IRH Press Co., Ltd.

IRH PRESS

New York . Tokyo

Distributed by National Book Network Inc. www.nbnbooks.com

Library of Congress Catalog Card Number: 2011915734

ISBN 13: 978-0-9826985-6-3
ISBN 10: 0-9826985-6-9

Printed in China

Cover Design: LeVan Fisher Design
Cover Photo Images: Shutterstock / DrHitch and Shutterstock / XONOVETS
Book Design: Jennifer Daddio/Bookmark Design & Media Inc.

CONTENTS

Chapter 3: The World of the Sixth Dimension

Chapter 4: The World of the Seventh Dimension

Chapter 5: The World of the Eighth Dimension

Chapter 6: The World of the Ninth Dimension

INTRODUCTION

The greatest thinkers and religious leaders throughout human history have all pondered the question of what happens after we die. Many have speculated on the possibility of an invisible world we go to in the afterlife and on what the existence of such a world might mean about the nature of our existence. However, no one has yet provided a complete description of this hidden world that awaits us beyond our last breath. Many religions teach us that there are a Heaven and a Hell in the other world, yet there is much about Heaven and Hell that we do not know.

How wonderful would it be if someone could describe God's intentions? If someone could show us what Heaven is like and what angels do, so that we may emulate them and join them in the next life? When we die, is it truly the end of this life as we know it? Is the final judgment so absolute that we truly are left to live eternally in either bliss or damnation? If angels and gods are not mere figments of the human imagination, then who are they, and what do they do? It is for lack of answers to these questions that people have feared death since the birth of humankind.

In *The Nine Dimensions*, Master Ryuho Okawa lifts away the veil that has kept the vast world beyond this one shrouded from our understanding. He describes in detail how God designed the world we see around us now, as well as the invisible but immeasurably vast and wondrous world that lies ahead of this temporary sojourn on Earth. Neither death nor Hell is anything to be feared, as long as you awaken to the Laws that God created and that are revealed within these very pages. Master Okawa shows us that we *can* make choices in life that will lead us to Heaven. This book is the surest gate to Heaven that anyone has ever placed before us.

Master Okawa's *The Nine Dimensions* reveals that, far from being the fearful and judging God that many religions so often depict, God is boundlessly merciful and loving. The true God, the Creator of our souls, never rests in His efforts to guide us as our Father. Time and again, He sends to Earth His closest envoys to teach God's Truths and to encourage us to pursue the attainment of spiritual happiness as we live within this material world. He is also our Mother, who out of compassion, created a system of eternal evolution called reincarnation to foster the growth of our souls by providing limitless opportunities to learn and progress, in stages, towards deeper awareness and higher enlightenment. This world and the other world were created as a school to nurture us and to guide us on the path to becoming greater angels.

As Master Okawa guides you through each of the dimensions, he reveals how our glorious God conceived a system to foster the eternal growth of our soul, a system that balanced two objectives: harmony and evolution. This world, the third dimension, and the spirit world from the fourth to the ninth dimensions, are based on spiritual Laws. God created these two worlds as a school that we go through, step by step, level by level, to grow closer to His likeness.

"Dimension" is a term Master Okawa uses to help describe a particular world that would otherwise be difficult to comprehend. In the first dimension, the only element that distinguishes beings from one another is length: this is the way you can distinguish one dot or line from another. In the second dimension, another element is added: width. Beings in this world are like flat sheets of paper. The third dimension has three elements—length, width, and height—which allows for a much more complex world of infinitely varying shapes and sizes. The third dimension is the world we live in now. In the fourth dimension, we enter a mysterious world whose inhabitants have attained a unique spiritual awareness that is shared by the other beings in that world.

In Chapter One, "The World of the Fourth Dimension,"

Master Okawa prepares us for what we will experience in the world immediately after our death, and encourages us to believe in the spiritual nature of our existence—to believe that we are not physical bodies, but souls. The fourth dimension is the world we will pass through as soon as our souls leave our corporeal garb. Here we determine which world, Heaven or Hell, we should move on to next. As you will discover, it is not God who sits in judgment, and you will also find out exactly how this determination is made.

In Chapter Two, "The World of the Fifth Dimension," Master Okawa shows us that God gave the spirit world (the other world) great diversity as well as order by creating many worlds layered horizontally and vertically. We will be divided into these different worlds based on our level of spiritual awareness and on which facets of God we focus on expressing. Souls who gather in the fifth dimension have awakened to their spirituality—they are aware that as children of God, they are characterized by goodness. Master Okawa also describes the experiences that we can only have as souls, and explains that the Laws behind how souls communicate are very different from those that determine how we communicate on Earth.

In Chapter Three, "The World of the Sixth Dimension," we find many spirits who are striving to improve their abilities as leaders in a specialized field. People in this dimension are not just any leaders, but are those who, in their various professions, have devoted themselves to learning God's Truths and inspiring others with God's words. In this chapter, you will find out more about God's intentions in creating a spiritual hierarchy, and why he wished to give diversity to humankind.

In Chapter Four, "The World of the Seventh Dimension," we enter the world of altruistic love. As we follow Master Okawa's description of the different forms of love that humans experience, we learn the essential nature of love, how it works, and the role it plays in giving human existence higher purpose and meaning. This dimension is filled with compassionate angels who have learned God's Truths deeply and are now devoted to actively spreading God's salvation far and wide. In these pages, you will discover exactly why God values love more highly than pure knowledge, and you will also find out what exactly God's love is.

In Chapter Five, "The World of the Eighth Dimension," Master Okawa shows us a world of towering figures who have appeared throughout history on God's behalf to elevate the spiritual progress of Earth's cultures to their highest peaks. You will also discover that God created the entire universe and all things within it, including the Laws, Truths, and our very souls, through three elements—light, space, and time—to achieve two key objectives: evolution balanced with harmony. You will learn that the secret to achieving lasting happiness lies in this objective.

In Chapter Six, "The World of the Ninth Dimension," Master Okawa pierces the cloud of mysticism to reveal the secret world of the greatest gods known to humankind, giving us a glimpse into a world that is almost beyond human comprehension. As you read about the origins of the most venerated religions and philosophies, you will draw closer to the heart of God's intentions. You will discover why He created so many religions around the world, as well as the best way to bring peace to religious and cultural conflicts.

You will see that God gave the universe diversity to make it more beautiful, and conceived the system of reincarnation to help us grow closer to His likeness, into greater angels. When we understand the world that surrounds us, both the invisible and the visible, and the Will of God that is imbued in it and in us, the answers to the age-old questions about life and the hereafter will appear right before us. Our longings will finally be satisfied.

About Master Okawa

In his homeland of Japan, Master Okawa is a well-known spiritual leader who has delivered more than 1,500 lectures throughout the country. He also travels abroad extensively to bring the words of God to people in all parts of the world; in recent years, he has spoken to audiences in New York, Los Angeles, London, Seoul, Hong Kong, New Delhi, Sydney, São Paulo, and more. People who have seen him speak are amazed by the dignity and power that emanate from his presence and his words. Moved by his love and compassion, many people come to see Master Okawa as the voice of Heaven.

Master Ryuho Okawa founded the Happy Science spiritual movement in 1986. He has published more than seven hundred books. He produced an incredible fifty-one store-released books in 2010 alone. His books are now available in twenty languages, including English, Spanish, Portuguese, French, Chinese, and Korean.

His Path to Spiritual Awakening

In 1981, at the age of twenty-four, Master Ryuho Okawa received revelations from Heaven from two revered Japanese Buddhist monks from the thirteenth century. The first of them, Nikko, announced to him through automatic writing that a gospel would be revealed soon. Nikko's message spelled out "good news, good news" in Japanese. The day this message was delivered, March 23, marked the start of Master Okawa's extraordinary path to the awakening of his deepest subconscious, and of his spiritual calling to deliver the words of God to the world. Shortly afterwards, Jesus Christ began speaking with Master Okawa, revealing that there was a huge and vitally important mission awaiting him.

Master Okawa's earlier years before embarking on this spiritual path could seem unusual for someone who is known today as the founder of a worldwide spiritual movement. He studied law at one of the top universities in Japan, The University of Tokyo, and started his first career in international trade. Between 1982 and 1983, he worked in offices located in the former World Trade Center in New York City while he took courses in international finance at the Graduate Center of the City University of New York.

Master Okawa's career in the financial district, chasing numbers day after day, posed a dramatic contrast to the spiritual life he was leading privately. By this time, many spirits from the highest parts of Heaven had been communicating with him frequently. While Master Okawa worked vigorously in the competitive world of business and trade, he spent much of his private time deepening his knowledge of the other world and learning from conversations with hundreds of Divine Spirits who appeared to speak with him. He spent more than five years learning from these angels and Divine Spirits about the intricacies of the spirit world and the essence of God's Truths.

His Understanding of God's Truths

This period of spiritual cultivation culminated in 1986. In June, Jesus Christ and other Divine Spirits came to Master Okawa with the message that the time had finally come, and entreated him to embark fully on his spiritual mission. He turned down a promotion at the trading company and walked away from his successful career, leaving the secular world behind. In August of that year, he wrote *The Laws of the Sun*, which revealed the extraordinary framework of God's Truths that would become the foundation of his teachings, which have grown to include more than seven hundred books today. The vast scale of Master Okawa's enlightenment was revealed in this first book and is the force that drives his spiritual movement forward to this very day.

The Laws of the Sun was not written with any intellectual preparation. What Master Okawa wrote emanated from the deepest parts of his consciousness; the words came from his own enlightenment and his understanding of God's Laws, which flowed from his mind to his fingers. Master Okawa, who had been a studious child and an avid reader since he was very small, was amazed himself to see that the words he had recorded surpassed the enlightenment of Shakyamuni Buddha and Jesus Christ.

Shortly after Jesus began conversing with Master Okawa in June 1981, the deepest parts of Master Okawa's own subconscious awakened. This was when he discovered his spiritual identity—that he is a soul named El Cantare, and that a part of this soul incarnated 2,500 years ago as Shakyamuni Buddha in India. Shakyamuni Buddha disclosed to Master Okawa from within his mind that his mission is to deepen his understanding of God's Truths to the fullest, and to deliver those words of salvation to the world. He learned that his soul is responsible for building and organizing the structure of God's Laws, and for delivering them in a comprehensible way, as teachings, to all people.

His Inner Training and Preparation

Several months before these spiritual revelations began in 1981, Master Okawa had been spending a lot of time in deep introspection, reflecting on his life to that point, and repenting for his errors and shortcomings. It was a period spent striving to discipline himself spiritually, purifying his mind, and finding gratitude for all those things he was blessed with and all the help and support he had received thus far. This practice of spiritual cleansing prepared his mind to unlock his subconscious, resulting in his enlightenment, and making him capable of speaking with Divine Spirits. Through that process, he discovered that it is not the mere act of meditating that leads to enlightenment. What leads to enlightenment is deeply poring over your life's words and deeds, becoming aware of who you are, and considering the qualities that meet with God's approval or disapproval. Master Okawa's enlightenment came from seeking God's Truths and pursuing self-awareness.

His Mission to Bring Peace to Religion

Since his great awakening in 1981, Master Okawa has spent many years recording and publishing messages from Divine Spirits. He continues to do so today, in hopes of showing that Heaven is a diverse place where many holy angels and the highest divinities work night and day to express aspects of God's multifaceted Truths. All the major world religions were derived from these divinities residing in the highest levels of Heaven.

Through his teachings, Master Okawa strives to reveal the purest and highest essence of God's Truths—the very source of all these religions—so that one day in humanity's bright future, the world's religions will forgive each other for their minor differences and acknowledge and accept one another. It is his deepest hope that his work will bring spiritual salvation to all people, bring people of every religion and nation together under faith in God, and inspire people to build a new era of harmony and peaceful progress.

PREFACE

I wrote this book, *The Nine Dimensions*, which reveals the doctrine of space, to complete the core trilogy of El Cantare's teachings. The first two volumes in the trilogy, *The Laws of the Sun* and *The Golden Laws*, discuss the structure of God's Laws and the doctrine of time, respectively, whereas this third book reveals the nature of space. When you read this book together with the other two books of the trilogy, you will be able to grasp the essential framework of the Laws of El Cantare.

Three large pillars support the structure of these Laws I teach. The first pillar is the vast system of God's Laws, including the universal Truths that govern all aspects of our lives. The second is the doctrine of time, which describes the roles and accomplishments of the Divine Spirits—angels, bodhisattvas, and tathagatas—that lived on Earth during the several thousand years of our recent history. The third pillar is the doctrine of space, which reveals a detailed description of the multidimensional structure of the other world, the world of our afterlife.

This book explores the third pillar, the world we enter after we leave this body. In these pages, I have summarized and explained the Eternal Truths that form the basis of that world, which encompasses this one, in a precise, logical way, for the first time in history. This book uncovers the long-hidden eternal mysteries of life. The ultimate secrets of Earth's spirit group, cloaked for so long by a veil of myth, are finally revealed.

I dedicate this book to the world with the earnest hope that it will help us surmount all difficulties and achieve the unification of all the religions in the world.

Ryuho Okawa
Founder and CEO
Happy Science Group
July 1997 (Japanese Edition)

THE WORLD
OF THE
FOURTH DIMENSION

1. This World and the Other World

"Where did I come from, and where will I go when I die?" This essential question always lingers somewhere in our minds, but very few people have been able to offer us credible answers. Unfortunately, as things now stand, the academic world has neither accumulated enough knowledge on the subject nor established a methodology that can provide us with viable explanations. There is far too little genuine understanding of the relationship between this world and the next.

The only clues we can find, faint as they may be, lie in the activities of psychic mediums who have appeared on Earth throughout the ages. But there are many kinds of mediums, and although some are trustworthy, most are not very reliable, much as we may want to put our faith in them. A psychic may claim to have spoken with a particular spirit, or may tell you that a certain event will happen in one year's time, but there is no way of verifying what he or she says. Even if the particular prediction comes to pass, it may just be coincidence. In the absence of tangible evidence, people are left feeling uncertain about the relationship between this world and the one that lies ahead.

If we could all have psychic experiences, nobody would doubt the existence of the other world. But, unfortunately, this ability is limited to only a few. As a result, many people are unaware of the existence of the other world. People who are generally considered "reasonable" tend not to believe in the existence of the other world, much less in the close connection between that world and this. Still, we continue to yearn for answers as we ponder the meaning of life in general and the reason for our own existence in particular.

We cannot find these answers until we know more about the truth of our existence in the vast universe. If, as materialists believe, life begins all of a sudden inside the mother's womb, continues for sixty or seventy years, and ends when we die, then we should live in a way that is appropriate to such a life. If, however, as many religious leaders claim, our souls come from another world and take physical form on Earth as part of an ongoing process of growth and evolution, then we need to adopt a very different perspective on life. In this world and in the spirit world to come, we want to live in ways that contribute to the ongoing improvement of our souls.

If we compare eternal life to formal education, life in this world is like elementary school. Even after we leave this world, we continue to learn in the other world, which, in spiritual terms, we might compare to middle school, high school, university and society. Materialists are like people who believe that education is over as soon as we graduate from elementary school; their perspective is so limited that they think there is nothing more we could possibly learn. On the other hand, people who believe that human beings have eternal souls and repeatedly reincarnate between this world and the other will be able to see Earth as a training ground for our souls and know that our spiritual education extends beyond this life.

When we look at life from these two opposing perspectives, it quickly becomes obvious which one leads to more progress for humanity: we achieve far more when we choose to believe that our souls evolve eternally through the cycle of reincarnation. Those who believe that life in this world is like the flame of a match, which flares up briefly only to disappear forever, will find it difficult, or even impossible, to discover the meaning of their lives. This short-term view is the very reason they choose to indulge in physical pleasures, blindly pursue material things, and see life only in terms of their own desires; it is only natural that they would want to enjoy themselves as much as possible if they believe they will vanish forever at the end of this fleeting life. Those who believe in eternal life, however, have a very different outlook. They develop their souls by serving others, knowing that when they benefit others, they are actually benefiting themselves.

As you can see, it is vital that you understand the relationship between this world and the other world when you contemplate the meaning and purpose of your life. Without this fundamental insight you will find it impossible to discover the truth about who you are.

2. The World of the Afterlife

We refer to the place we go when we die—after the soul is separated from the physical body—as the "other world." But what kind of place is this other world? What awaits us after death? Because most of us don't know what to expect, we develop a strong attachment to our life in this world. If you were to ask one hundred people whether they would like to die, ninety-nine would probably answer no—not because they enjoy living in this world so much, but because they fear what might happen afterward. There are also some people, as we know, who find life in this world so unbearable that they overcome this fear of the unknown and take their own lives.

Although these people—those who fear death and those who would rather take their own lives than suffer in this world—have very different perspectives, they overlap in one significant way: both groups of people are basically uninformed about the other world, the world we go to after we die. If you knew, for example, that you had to sail across the sea without good charts to show the way, you would understandably feel uneasy. But if you had proper maps, and were oriented to where you came from and where you were heading, you could make the journey without concern. I believe it is my mission to explain what happens in the other world clearly, and to guide people across to the other shore.

When we are faced with death, few people want to accept it. Patients in hospitals generally say they do not wish to die, and doctors do everything in their power to extend their patients' lives. But if we could see death from the perspective of the other world, we would discover our guardian spirits, Guiding Spirits, and other angels gathering around our deathbeds. Even before the moment of death arrives, these spirits are already preparing to guide us through our transition.

So what does happen when we die? As I have mentioned in various books and lectures, our lives are not limited to our physical lifespan in this world: the soul continues to exist through this world and the next. When the end of this life finally comes, the soul moves out of the physical body, although at first you don't even realize what is happening; it feels as if you have two separate bodies—one lying in bed and the other moving about freely. But when you, in the body that moves around freely, try to communicate with the people surrounding you, you will find yourself being completely ignored. To your astonishment, you discover that you can pass through walls and other material objects. Because you still believe that you are the body lying in bed, you continue to hover over it, which leads to an even greater shock when you see your body being taken to the crematorium or the funeral parlor. Not knowing what to do, you wander around near your coffin, uncertain and nervous about what will happen next.

This is the moment when your guardian spirit appears and begins to explain what is going on. If you didn't believe in the existence of the world of the afterlife while you lived on Earth, it will be difficult at first for you to understand what the guardian spirit is telling you. In this case you will most likely remain on Earth for several weeks, until your guardian spirit can help you accept what has taken place.

Buddhist services for the dead are held on the seventh and forty-ninth days after death. This is because the spirit of a person who has just died is generally allowed to remain on Earth for some twenty to thirty days. During this transitional period, the spirit receives instruction from its guardian spirits and Guiding Spirits on how to return to the other world. Those whose attachment to this world on Earth is too great, however, are unable to leave. For instance, those who are obsessed with and cling to their children, father, mother, wife, husband, or even their land, house, wealth, or business, will become what are known as "Earth-bound spirits" that wander about in this world, or what people usually think of as "ghosts." Unaware of the fact that they are spirits, they still think that the physical body is the true self.

3. Memories of Having a Physical Body

Most people suffer some degree of shock and confusion when they first find themselves in the other world, but as time passes, they become used to living there. At first they find it surprising that they can go indefinitely without having to eat or drink, but gradually they realize that they no longer need a physical body. Eventually, after confirming that they cannot be seen or heard by those who remain on Earth, these new spirits stop trying to communicate with the friends and family they have left behind.

As they cast off their old habits and realize that they are spiritual beings, new arrivals to the spirit world gradually acquire a different way of looking at things—and gain a "spiritual sense." They discover that they can float on air, pass through solid objects, and travel vast distances instantaneously. If they want to visit someone, they can travel hundreds of kilometers in the blink of an eye just by thinking to themselves, "I want to say goodbye to that person," or "I would like to see my friend one last time." They find these experiences thrilling at first, but soon get used to them.

Most spirits settle down after exploring their new surroundings and their place in them, much the way a child does after entering school for the first time and being confronted with that completely new world. Usually, memories of life on Earth start to fade away, although for some spirits, the memories remain fresh and may even become more vivid. Newly-arrived spirits, then, can be sorted into two groups: those who remember their life on Earth less and less, and those who cling to their memories of Earth-bound existence.

At some point, most of those spirits still wandering around on Earth are guided by their deceased friends or relatives or by their guardian spirits to a "reception center" in the fourth dimension[1] (known as the Posthumous World), where people go right after they die. Here they actively review and reflect on their lives on Earth. The focus of this intro-

---

[1] The fourth dimension is divided into the Astral Realm and the realm of Hell. In our afterlife, after our souls leave our physical bodies, we will go through a process that determines whether we will head to the Astral Realm or Hell.

spection is mistakes they have made, which become clear now that they can see their lives from the spirit world; this is the time when the recently deceased must look back at their way of life and consider how much of it was centered on material desire.

Upon reflection, those who realize that their life was driven by physical desires without spiritual consideration can elect to go to Hell, which exists in the lower part of the fourth dimension. In Hell they will face specific ordeals based on their misguided thoughts and actions on Earth— tribulations that will serve as further spiritual training. Even if you did live a life driven by physical desires, however, if you recognize the mistakes you made, and truly repent of your wrongdoing, you may avoid choosing Hell and go on to the Astral Realm, which is in the upper part of the fourth dimension where harmonized spirits live[2].

When souls arrive in the Astral Realm, they see beings they had never seen before. They encounter the kinds of creatures that are mentioned in ancient tales, such as dragons, water sprites, and small fairy-like beings that fly around in flower gardens. Many beings that we consider mythical can be found in the Astral Realm, and by observing them, new-

---

[2] The Astral Realm in the fourth dimension somewhat resembles what we usually think of as Heaven. This is where people go to get used to being spiritual beings without physical bodies. After spending some time in the Astral Realm, those who attain a higher level of awareness will gradually move on to higher dimensions.

comers gradually deepen their understanding of the workings of the spirit world.

As you can see, memories of our time on Earth help determine our future lives. There is no omnipotent being who
sits in judgment over us; rather it is our own conscience, our
true nature as children of God, that chooses what comes next.
After consulting with our guardian spirit, if we feel that we
need more spiritual discipline, we are the ones who elect to
go to Hell for further training. Although we make the choice
to go to Hell ourselves, some people forget this fact after
spending many years in Hell, and gradually come to think
that they are being punished. There are also cases in which
extremely vicious souls are cast straight to Hell immediately
after they die, without going through the self-selection process. You may think of them as the gangsters and violent
offenders of the other world, who have no choice but to go
directly to spiritual boot camp.

4. *The Roles of Angels*

These days, most people have difficulty believing that angels
and devils exist outside fairy tales and dismiss the notion
with a laugh. Although Christianity is based on "the Father,
the Son, and the Holy Spirit," many Christians seem to have
difficulty accepting angels as manifestations of the Holy

Spirit. Even devout Christians who accept the existence of the angels described in the Bible can be uncomfortable believing in them as actual entities. However, angels really do exist, as do devils, which is why stories about them can be found throughout history in both the East and the West and in advanced as well as developing countries.

The word *angel* refers to Divine Spirits at various spiritual levels. Those known as angels come from the upper part of the sixth dimension and above. These are the divinities that we have recognized throughout history as saints and gods when they have taken human form. The Divine Spirits that reside in the seventh and eighth dimensions, known as bodhisattvas and tathagatas respectively, are also angels.

At their initial level of training, angels become responsible for people who have just departed from the three-dimensional world. At this stage, angels are engaged in the practical tasks of saving souls. They act as guides for people who have just left their bodies, looking after them and educating them. These angels number in the hundreds of millions, and change their appearance according to the ideology, beliefs, and religion of the deceased. Angels from the Christian spirit group generally look after and guide Christians, bodhisattvas from the Buddhist spirit group provide guidance to Buddhists, and so on. These angels appear in whatever form makes it easy for the recently deceased to accept them.

Angels not only exist in the other world, but also live

in this one. Most angels reincarnate on Earth repeatedly, although the frequency of their reincarnation varies widely, from every few hundred years to every thousand years[3]. They are born here for the purpose of training their souls and purifying the world, but they also come down to Earth to remind themselves what it is like to live as human beings. If they remain in the other world for too long, it becomes difficult for them to understand how people on Earth think or feel. So in order to become better teachers of souls, angels need to come down to Earth periodically and take on human form. An added advantage of being born on Earth in this way is that by understanding human sensibilities, they are able to preach God's Truths to a wide variety of people while still giving each person the specific teachings they need. This allows them to lead as many people as possible to salvation.

As I mentioned earlier, the first thing that people experience after death is the presence of angels. For Christians, these angels appear with wings; they take on the garb of monks for Buddhists; and they appear in the robes of priests before believers in Shinto. No matter what kind of appearance they take, all angels shine brightly, and their heads are crowned by a dazzling halo. Deep within our souls, we all believe in the

---

[3] As a basic rule, all human beings reincarnate in this world, including angels and even those who have fallen to Hell in the past, provided that they repent their wrongdoing and return to Heaven before being born on Earth.

existence of divinities. Even people who claimed while they lived on Earth that God didn't exist quickly put their hands together in prayer when faced with an angel.

5. A New Beginning

No matter how great or how immature a spirit you may be, once you are conceived in the mother's womb and born into this world, you lose your memories of the spirit world and your past lives, and experience a new beginning. You have to start from zero. In the same way, after spending a lifetime studying on Earth, souls graduate from this world and move on to a new school called the other world. Just as they did when they were born on Earth, these souls make a new start: they meet new teachers, and they learn new lessons.

New arrivals to the spirit world take an intensive course on the meaning of spirituality from angels, or from old friends, or from teachers who have arrived in the other world ahead of them. This lesson provides these spirits with important guidelines for their future life in the other world. Although many of them will forget what they learned after they have settled down to their new lives, they do receive guidance at the first stage of their transition.

As we've seen, some of the souls who arrive in the other world will depart for Hell. Before we explore this further, it's important to note that Hell is not equal in size to Heaven. Heaven stretches from the fourth to the ninth and tenth dimensions or beyond, whereas Hell occupies only a tiny place in the other world—the lower part of the fourth dimension—so in no way is it equal to the size of Heaven.

There are all kinds of people living in this world here on Earth. A certain number are sick, so we have doctors and hospitals to treat them. In much the same way, there are souls in the other world who are spiritually sick, and for them Hell is like a hospital where they undergo rehabilitation. I ask you to bear in mind that although these souls may be sick, they are struggling to learn, and therefore to heal themselves. You may be able to teach healthy people how to drive a car, ride a bicycle, jump, or run in long distance races, but sick people may not be capable of any of these things. First, they may need to learn how to use crutches, or practice walking while somebody supports them. Sick people need training and education that best addresses their needs, and the same holds true for sick spirits.

6. The Destinations of Our Souls

Souls that have just left their physical bodies cannot adapt to their new spiritual existence right away. It's not easy to get used to life as a spiritual being after spending a lifetime on Earth. For one thing, people have difficulty getting used to how it feels not to have a physical body. When we are alive and we want something nearby, we can just reach out and pick it up. But souls that have left their bodies can no longer hold on to anything in the material world, and at first they find this very frustrating. Before too long, however, even those spirits who do not realize that they are dead begin to take aspects of their new state for granted. Then it comes time to decide whether to take the road that leads to Heaven or the one that leads to Hell.

The most important factor that determines whether you will go to Heaven or Hell is what kind of person you were before you died. In other words, to make a choice you have to know your true nature; this becomes the guideline for the kind of life you will lead in the next world. How should we live on Earth in order to return to Heaven, and what kind of life on Earth will lead us to Hell? Today very few people can provide clear answers to these questions. Even if we believe in the existence of the other world, we cannot always be certain whether we are living in a way that will lead us to Heaven or Hell.

The simplest way of predicting our destination—and the most popular way throughout thousands of years of history all around the world—is to check whether our past actions were sinful or innocent according to religious edicts. The most famous of these edicts are probably the Ten Commandments of Moses and the Code of Hammurabi in Mesopotamia, both of which were originally based on teachings of higher spirits, the Guiding Spirits of Light[4]. But because their full message was difficult to understand, those teachings were recast in the form of simple commandments that prohibited some actions and encouraged others. For most people, including those aware of the existence of the spirit world, it is easier to assess whether they will to go to Heaven or Hell if they review their lives in accordance with these spiritual rules. Many of the rules of conduct we follow today, as well as many laws that govern our lives, originate from these religious commandments.

Commandments definitely provide a basic, clear guide to right and wrong. "Thou shalt not kill" and "Thou shalt not steal" imply that if you transgress in these ways, you are more likely to go to Hell, and if you do not, you are more likely to go to Heaven. Although this simple system definitely has value and importance, it is not the only determining factor in choosing our destination. In fact, a broader guideline may

---

[4.] Guiding Spirits of Light are spirits that reside in the seventh dimension (the World of Bodhisattvas) and the eighth dimension (the World of Tathagatas). These spirits receive vast quantities of God's light and spread this light to people, giving them guidance and hope. They reincarnate on Earth every few hundred to few thousand years to enlighten people and lead them to spiritual awakening, often through religious activities.

be even more useful: Those who become aware during their life on Earth of their true nature as children of God ascend to Heaven, and the more they manifest their true nature, the higher the level of Heaven to which they return. On the other hand, those who do not awaken to their true nature as children of God, and show no sign of growth in their lifetime on Earth, are likely to face ordeals in Hell after they leave this world.

7. The Unknown World

You may or may not have given much thought to Hell during your life on Earth, but if you were actually to be faced with Hell, you would be shocked by its horrors. There are various types of Hell, some of them inhabited by devils and demon-like creatures as much as thirteen feet tall, and others by demons who seem to be attacking you with knives in their hands. In the Hell of Lust, people writhe in a sea of blood, while in the Hell of Hungry Spirits, people who appear to be nothing but skin and bones stagger around like famine victims, crying out for something to eat. Residents of the Hell of Beasts no longer look human. As described in a novel by the famous Japanese writer Ryunosuke Akutagawa (1892-1927), souls who have fallen into the Hell of Beasts may have the bodies of horses, oxen, or pigs, but with human faces.

There are other souls who take on the bodies of snakes and slither across the ground.

These poor souls do not know why they are in their present state; in fact, they ended up taking these forms because they were unaware of their true nature as spiritual beings. These people also did not know that their secret thoughts on Earth would manifest in the next world, for in the spirit world your thoughts become reality. They believed that just because their thoughts could not be seen from the outside during life on Earth, they could think whatever they liked. If their thoughts had been visible to those around them while they were living in the flesh, they would have been ashamed to appear in public. Imagine the shock they must feel now that they have changed into a shape that conforms to what they think, visible for all to see!

We would all realize the mistakes in our hearts right away if, for example, we turned into snakes because of our envious thoughts or the grudges we carry. But since this is not possible in this world we live in, we often remain unaware of our mistakes. In the other world, however, thoughts actualize instantly. A person whose thoughts are constantly filled with desire for the opposite sex will fall into the Hell of Lust, where he or she must constantly seek sexual satisfaction. Cunning people who lived to deceive and cheat others will find themselves taking the shape of a fox in the other world. Those filled with envy and hatred will turn into snakes. These are only a few examples, but I'm sure you get the idea.

These spirits can seek temporary respite from the agonies of Hell by possessing people on Earth. However, they cannot possess just anybody they choose; they can only possess those who have already created a Hell within themselves through their own thoughts. Those who have created a Hell of Lust within their minds may attract the inhabitants of the Hell of Lust. Those who create a Hell of Beasts in their minds may be possessed by spirits that look like animals. Those whose ideas are wrong from a true religious or ideological perspective and lead others down the wrong path create an abysmal hell within their own minds and may be possessed by those who have already fallen into the appropriately named Abysmal Hell. In short, Hell exists within our own inner worlds too, and the spirits from Hell in the other world can only enter and possess those of us who have already created a similar Hell in our own minds.

8. Eternal Life of the Soul

Spirits suffering in Hell can often be heard saying, "I would rather die than continue my life like this." They curse God or Buddha, saying, "It would be better if you had killed me straight out instead of making me live like a snake," or "Why don't you put me out of my misery? Anything would be better than trying to stay afloat in this sea of blood." Inhabitants of the Abysmal Hell, trapped in darkness or the desert, or sealed into caves, moan, "If this is all the life that remains to me, why couldn't you just put an end to it?"

Through the use of my second sight, I have seen many cases where a guru of a renowned religious organization who received high praise in this world suffers all alone in the infinite darkness of swamps in the Abysmal Hell. Some of these fallen spiritual leaders are founders of religions that have lasted for generations. They cannot understand how they could find themselves in such a terrible situation when once they enjoyed tens of thousands, even millions of follow-ers. They would much rather seek oblivion than continue on their present course, which gives us insight into the terrible power of uncertainty: because these fallen spiritual leaders have no idea how much longer they must suffer, trapped in impenetrable darkness, their pain is all the more difficult to bear.

This suffering is compounded by the fact that souls are eternal. The fact that there is life after death is the ultimate blessing for those who have lived a harmonious life with pure hearts: they can continue to enjoy their happiness in Heaven. However, life in the next world is itself a horrible punishment and castigation for those who have fallen into Hell. Unfortu-nately for them, life does not end when they lose their physical bodies; on the contrary, it stretches out, and this very fact serves to punish them further.

Once you understand the workings of the other world, it quickly becomes obvious that you do yourself harm by having evil thoughts and by acting on them in this world. Those who do not believe that the soul continues to exist, and instead think that life ends when they die, might not care if they hurt others through words or actions as long as they can become rich and powerful. As a result, they are shocked when they fall down into Hell and face agony instead of the blessings of eternal harmony.

When you discover that a life of goodness, even a modest one, leads to a life of unparalleled bliss in the world beyond this one, you will regret that you didn't do more good while you were alive. One act of kindness in this world increases its value tenfold in the next, but this is precisely because life in this world is very difficult; it is as if the soul goes through life blindfolded. If we manage to keep a heavenly state of mind while groping our way forward in this world, then that hard-won spiritual discipline will be worth five or ten times more in the other world.

In the same way, small misdeeds that seem unimportant in this life will also be repaid five or tenfold. If you are repeatedly involved in wrongdoing, you will face a difficult situation in the next life. If you care about yourself in the truest sense, you know that you have no choice but to do good and not evil, for your own sake. You will do good not because you want to receive praise or because you feel obligated to follow an earthly moral code, but because you know that what you do in this life will be repaid in the next life. Evil simply does not pay.

Ironically, the kinds of people who end up in Hell are the very ones who in life would have hated more than anything to put themselves at a disadvantage relative to others. Because of their ignorance, they do not realize that their selfish approach does just that. Enlightened self-interest is a powerful tool, which is why it is so important that we spread God's Truths as soon as possible.

9. Recalling Our Past Lives

In this chapter I have revealed various facts about Heaven and Hell, but one of the most surprising and exciting experiences for souls returning to the fourth dimension is that here we can recall memories from our previous lives. In the third dimension, we are born, become an adult, and eventually grow old. Whatever we learn is limited to the experience we gain through the course of our lives. However, when we return to the next world, we realize that our true lifetime was not limited to this past life, or even to the past thousands or tens of thousands of years. Our souls contain the memories of tens of millions, even hundreds of millions of years. When we return to the other world, these memories come back, and we realize that we have been living for time immemorial.

Those in Hell, however, find it difficult to recall past lives. Life in Hell is a painful, grueling experience, and when one is in great agony it is difficult to reflect on anything, including the past. If you were suffering from a severe toothache, it would not be easy for you to recall a particular memory. The same is true for spirits writhing in the agonies of Hell. Although theoretically they are capable of recalling events from their previous lives, it is virtually impossible for them to do so.

On the other hand, those who have returned to Heaven can readily recall their previous lives, although the extent to which they can do so varies according to their spiritual ability. Those who lived an ordinary life may remember one or two previous lives at the most and only have a vague memory of something before that. However, as they evolve to become spirits in higher dimensions, they begin to remember their past lives more vividly and completely. It's a bit like climbing an observation tower. The higher the tower, the more you can see when you go up to the top. If the observation deck is only a few stories high, you will only be able to see what's going on nearby, and if you go down to the basement, it will be impossible to see anything outside at all. Hell is like that basement from which you can't see anything outside. In terms of your memory, the higher the dimension you ascend to, the further back you can remember.

Bodhisattvas, or spirits in the seventh dimension, can remember their lives for tens of thousands of years. Tathagatas in the eighth dimension can remember even further into the past, recalling things that happened as many as hundreds of thousands, or even millions of years ago. When a spirit reaches the level of the Grand Tathagata in the ninth dimension, it can recall every single event, from how it came into existence hundreds of millions of years ago, to how the Earth was formed, to how humankind has evolved since then. It can recall the very beginning of time.

In sum, although we all remember our previous lives when we go back to the spirit world, the extent to which this can be achieved depends very much on the individual. Some people can remember only their most recent previous life, others can go back several lives, and some may be able to cast their minds back over hundreds of previous existences. This is indeed a wondrous aspect of the spirit world. As you cultivate your spiritual awareness, you will be able to widen your vistas in all directions, including the past, the present, and the future.

10. Our Path through Evolution

So far, I have been describing various aspects of the fourth dimension, that is to say, preparing you for what you will experience after you leave this three-dimensional world. But you may be asking yourself more fundamental questions. You may be wondering, "Why do I have to go through these experiences? Why do Heaven and Hell exist? Why are we not made aware of them while we are still alive? Why do we have a body and a spirit? Why can't we just live as a spirit in this world too?"

The transition from the body to the spirit can be compared to the metamorphosis of the cicada or the butterfly. After many years of living underground, the cicada nymph climbs a tree, clings to the trunk, casts off its skin, and then flies off into the sky. A green caterpillar crawling across a leaf will one day pupate and become a dazzling butterfly. God created this life cycle of cicadas and butterflies to teach human beings about the cycle of reincarnation. In the same way that the insect changes its form, we evolve spiritually as we reincarnate between this world and the spirit world. The transformation a caterpillar makes, from an awkward creature with dozens of stubby legs, gorging itself on a leaf, to a butterfly fluttering freely across the sky, provides us with a clue to the spiritual evolution of humankind.

Why did God create this kind of system, when He could just as easily have made butterflies free to fly from birth? It is an example of His compassion. By experiencing the limitations of an earth-bound life, we will more fully appreciate just how miraculous it is when we are able to fly. God wants us to know that this transcendent joy awaits us in the spirit world. You may not wish to be born a butterfly, but you can imagine the kind of joy that butterflies experience as they flutter freely across the sky. God granted butterflies a kind of happiness that human beings cannot experience in this life, which is another example of God's compassion, this time for butterflies.

Our souls are constrained by these physical bodies now, but eventually we will shed them. That is when we will fully realize how wonderful it is to be a spiritual being. In this material world of the third dimension, it takes time for our wishes to come true, so we can feel frustrated, exhausted, and incompetent. In the spirit world, our thoughts manifest instantly. When we return to that world after spending a lifetime struggling in the third dimension, we appreciate it even more.

Through the system of reincarnation, God provides us with a path to spiritual evolution. Without going through this spiritual metamorphosis—this elevation to the next stage—we cannot experience true happiness. As spiritual beings, we have essentially the same nature as that of God. It is absolutely incredible to be able to manifest God's nature in ourselves, and this experience is a process that begins in this wonderful world in which we live.

Even if we suffer through centuries in Hell, in the long term, this experience serves as a whetstone for refining the soul. We have placed ourselves in an environment where we have no choice but to face our shortcomings and concentrate on correcting them. Those spirits dwelling in Hell, therefore, cannot be simply written off as evil; they too are walking the path to spiritual evolution.

This is not to say, however, that spirits should be left in Hell unaided. They do experience great pain, so we must guide them to realize the mistakes they made and lead them in the correct direction. This is the way it should be, in accordance with God's Will, which is why God constantly sends angels to help those who suffer in Hell. But even if spirits in Hell choose not to rely on outside help, the very fact of their being in Hell provides them an opportunity to realize on their own where they have gone wrong. It may seem like a backward step, but in the eternity that is the life of a soul, it is just another part of the path to spiritual evolution.

WHAT HAPPENS
IN THE AFTERLIFE
BEFORE REINCARNATION?

•

The spirits who have just arrived in the fourth dimension are like novice drivers until they get used to the workings of the spirit world. It takes quite a long time for them to master the laws of the spirit world, and they spend about three years at each dimension before moving up to the next higher dimension.

Some of these new spirits are fully satisfied with what the fourth dimension has to offer. They say, "I can fly, I can walk under water, what more could I want?" And before long, these spirits are reborn on Earth again. Others, however, possess a higher spiritual awareness and are not satisfied with the fourth dimension. These spirits enjoy being reunited with their old teachers and primary school classmates, but they gradually realize that they are seeking something different from what the others are seeking.

When the time comes, a Guiding Spirit comes down from a higher dimension to take each spirit to the level that is best suited to that spirit's development. After a spirit has remained at its new level for a while, the day comes when it has to set off again and head for an even higher dimension.

The higher one goes, the more there is to learn, but eventually, all spirits reach their limit and realize that they are not capable of progressing any further. When they realize this, they are reborn again on Earth.

How long people stay in the spirit world depends on the level of their spiritual awareness, and therefore, the interval between different people's incarnations varies considerably.

2

THE WORLD
OF THE
FIFTH DIMENSION

1. *The World of Goodness*

In chapter I, we learned about the first world we enter when we cast off our physical bodies and return to our spiritual form; in this chapter, you'll find out what it's like in the dimension immediately beyond that. The latest research in theoretical physics considers the world we live in now to be part of a multilayered structure consisting of many dimensions. The third dimension is enveloped by the fourth, the fourth by the fifth, and so on—each higher dimension encompasses those below it to create a vast, onion-like entity.

If you could visit the spirit world, as I can, you would

discover that this description of the spirit world is accurate to the tiniest detail. Contrary to what many believe, the spirits in the fourth dimension do not live in a world completely separated from our world on Earth. They coexist with the incarnated souls in the third dimension and exert various influences over them. The fifth dimension interacts with the fourth and lower dimensions in much the same way, and so on. This is a universal principle that runs through the other world; the inhabitants of higher dimensions can influence people on lower planes, but not the other way around. For example, residents of the fifth dimension are free to travel to the fourth dimension, where they can offer guidance to people there, but, with very few exceptions, the inhabitants of the fourth dimension cannot visit the fifth.

This spiritual hierarchy in the other world is accepted by Buddhism, mysticism, and theosophy and is confirmed in numerous ancient manuscripts. These writings state that the spiritual universe is not merely divided into two parts—this world on Earth and the spirit world—but that the other world is itself made up of many different realms layered both horizontally and vertically. Emanuel Swedenborg, the famous eighteenth-century European mystic and psychic, made numerous visits to the spirit world and documented what he saw there. His notes indicate that when you look up in the spirit world, you can see what appears to be a transparent veil that covers the sky and seems to divide this world from the one above it. In truth, this veil is not visible, but Swedenborg was correct in noticing that there was another world beyond the one he was in. There definitely are separate but overlapping worlds arranged in layers above each other.

All this said, what is the difference between the fourth and fifth dimensions? As we've seen, the fourth dimension is the first world we encounter when we step into the spirit world. Its inhabitants are in some ways like small children in school for the very first time because they have yet to gain a full understanding of the relationship between the body and the spirit, between physical matter and the soul. Because these souls still retain many of the behaviors and customs they had on Earth, the lifestyles they live in the fourth dimension are a mixture of both earthly and spiritual ways of life. However, after living in the fourth dimension for a while, these souls begin to evolve. Some require only a few days or months to do so, while others need decades or even centuries, but once they are ready, their guardian spirits, Guiding Spirits, or angels come to lead them up to the fifth dimension.

If I had to sum up the difference between the fourth and fifth dimensions in one word, I would describe it as "goodness." In the fifth dimension, you will find that all the inhabitants are souls with a strong, natural disposition towards goodness who have made a conscious choice to pursue good and abandon evil. They are also aware, to some extent, that goodness is a quality that God seeks from us.

2. A Spiritual Awakening

Goodness in the fifth dimension is not just virtue as we know it, or the opposite of evil; it is born of an awareness of being a child of God, and is the very expression of this divine nature within us. To put it another way, this goodness is rooted in spiritual awakening.

On Earth, the material and spiritual aspects of our lives live side by side. When we engage with the material world, we worry about everyday worldly necessities, such as making a living and buying, using, and replacing material things. Those of us who become aware of the other aspect of life, and spend evenings or weekends engaged in things that give us spiritual joy, feel very fortunate and are regarded by society as people of great character and integrity. Of course, some people never experience any spiritual pleasure, immersing themselves instead in gambling and other worldly pleasures, but most of us do not find this satisfying; instead we feel drawn to more spiritual pursuits, such as reading, music, or art. This attraction comes from a subconscious longing for the world from which we came.

The fifth dimension is often referred to as "the World of Goodness" or "the World of Spirituality," and all its inhabitants are highly aware that we are all spiritual beings. By contrast, those who have not yet elevated from the fourth dimension, or the Posthumous World, have not yet reached a complete understanding of our spiritual nature—that at the very essence of our being, we are souls. Nor have they devoted themselves to the pursuit of the goodness that lies within them.

Once people reach the fifth dimension, however, they are fully aware that our true nature is the soul, and they are totally committed to the quest for goodness. Belief in religion is also something they all share, though this belief need not be very strong. Their personal philosophies still reflect their religious background—they may believe in God, or Buddha, or Allah, for example—but they all share a basic belief in some form of deity. And by now, they feel that God is close at hand and live their lives for His sake.

You may be surprised to find people in the fifth dimension working at the same kinds of jobs that we perform here on Earth. You will see merchants, construction workers, and people of many other professions, including those who work in what we on Earth refer to as the service industries. The big difference is that in the fifth dimension, no one works in order to earn money. Instead, they are motivated by a desire to please God: this has become their principal source of pleasure.

LIFE
IN THE
FIFTH DIMENSION

•

The fifth dimension, or the World of Goodness, is a world that good-natured, harmonious people return to in the afterlife. The inhabitants continue their spiritual discipline in human form for about 90 percent of the time. But through occasional mysterious experiences, they begin to realize that they are not the same as they believed themselves to be; they have no need to walk on the ground, and even if they jump off a cliff, they will not die. They begin to realize that they have the ability to move freely to any place they wish.

In the fourth dimension, souls under the guidance of various spirits occasionally appear wherever they want or meet whomever they wish, but these experiences happen only by chance. In the fifth dimension, souls are able to do this more or less at will. They begin to realize through their own experiences that they can exist without a human form, and they become aware that they are actually spiritual beings. They are still concerned about their physical bodies, however, and do not feel comfortable if, for example, they are not the same height as they were while on Earth.

3. Experiencing the Joy of the Soul

Inhabitants of the fourth dimension cannot fully appreciate the *joy* of the soul. Instead, they experience what is known as *amazement* of the soul—they are still experiencing the novelty of discovering that they are, in fact, souls, and can experience wondrous things in their new form. People of the Posthumous World have yet to differentiate fully between life in the fourth dimension and life on Earth, and they are still clothed in a form of corporal garb known as the "astral body." The astral body is a more spiritual form of the physical body, but it is not as spiritually pure as the soul. The astral body has a strong connection with the physical body and houses the "consciousness" of each of our internal organs, whereas the soul is where our overall consciousness resides. When a soul advances into the World of Goodness in the fifth dimension, the astral body that protects the soul is cast away; everyone in the fifth dimension lives in their more spiritually refined soul form, and as a result, residents of the fifth dimension are capable of experiencing the true joy of the soul.

So what kind of joy does the soul feel, and when? First, the soul feels joy when it is able to bring people joy by helping others. We experience the same kind of joy on Earth. When someone says to us, "I am so glad you are here," or "Thanks to you, things went very well," we feel appreciated for the efforts we have made on behalf of other people. In these moments of delight, we are able to affirm the goodness and the virtuousness within us. We realize that we are not living for ourselves alone. When other people benefit from our good deeds, we experience the effect of our contributions extending far beyond the limits of our own, individual lives. Whenever this happens, our souls experience the joy of expansion and self-improvement; this spiritual growth multiplies the value of our single existence many times over. One of the best ways to experience joy of the soul is to bring joy to those around us.

The second way our souls experience joy is when we discover something new. This is not the kind of knowledge found in school, but the kind we gain when we discover something profound about the wondrous world that God has created. To put it another way, this is spiritual knowledge. Every time we make a breakthrough, our soul is filled with joy. The soul has many inherent traits and abilities that the inhabitants of the fifth dimension do not fully appreciate, but through the experiences they have, they gradually become aware of these qualities. Let me provide an example.

As we've seen, people in the fifth dimension still work at various jobs, such as farming. Of course they are aware that eating is no longer necessary for sustenance, but enjoying a good meal—or in this case the satisfaction of growing food for others to enjoy—still gives them great pleasure. However, over time, they realize that they don't have to do these familiar things to feel joy—that there is such a thing as a purely spiritual form of happiness. They gradually become more aware that this is the true state of their existence. Although they may be growing potatoes, these are not potatoes in the physical, three-dimensional sense; they are spiritual potatoes, which have their origins in the mind. On Earth, advancements in science continue to contribute all kinds of improvements to modern agriculture, but this is not necessary in the other world, where anyone can grow beautiful crops, vibrant with nutrients, as long as you give your garden heartfelt love and attention. In time, these farmers in the fifth dimension come to realize that the richer and fuller their minds become, the more beautiful are the potatoes they produce. These farmers learn a very fundamental principle that applies throughout the spiritual world: that their very thoughts manifest as reality. The acquisition of this spiritual knowledge, then, is the second form of joy experienced in this world.

4. The Flow of Light

I'd like to explore the theme of spiritual knowledge a little further. As we've seen, the people of the fourth dimension are not yet fully aware that the essence of our souls was formed from the light that came from God. Those who have moved on to the fifth dimension, however, are souls who have begun to discover the true nature of this light; they become aware of the presence of a form of light that does not come from candles or light fixtures, and they find that they are capable of distinguishing variations in the intensity of this light. They have discovered a form of light that comes from God, and realize that they are drawing energy from His light. In time, they will see that the source of this energy is the Spiritual Sun that is lighting up their sky—the spirit-world equivalent of the sun that sustains life on Earth.

What exactly is this Spiritual Sun? What is its true nature? The Spiritual Sun is the spiritual body, or soul, of the sun that everyone sees on Earth. Just as an individual soul resides inside the human body, a great soul known as Earth Consciousness resides within Earth's planetary body, and the same is true of the sun. Inside the physical sun that shines its material light down on Earth dwells a Spiritual Sun that emanates *spiritual* light.

Thus, the sun of the third dimension that we see every

day is not only giving us valuable heat and light energy to sustain all *physical* forms of life on Earth, but is also continuously delivering *spiritual* energy to the other world. Earth is one of many planets in our solar system, all of which are governed by the great solar system consciousness that supplies these planets with precious life-sustaining energy.

The sun's spirit—its body of spiritual energy—is the stellar consciousness of our solar system and is called the Solar System Consciousness; it resides in the eleventh dimension. From the eleventh dimension, the Solar System Consciousness delivers to Earth seven colors of light by sending its energy through the three tenth-dimensional planetary consciousnesses of the Grand Sun Consciousness, the Moon Consciousness, and the Earth Consciousness. From there, this energy is passed on to the ten spirits residing in the ninth dimension, who further diffuse the light and distribute it to two places: this world on Earth and the other world.

Although the souls of the fifth dimension do not know all this, they are aware that the Spiritual Sun provides them with the essential energy that gives them life, much the way the physical sun does for Earth's three-dimensional residents. Because they are aware of this fact, the inhabitants of the World of Goodness are in touch with their gratitude to the Spiritual Sun before they develop even the simplest forms of faith in God. In the early morning and evening, they can often be found praying outdoors, hands clasped in reverence as they watch the way the Sun's spiritual light flows and spreads around them. As I've described in this section, the fifth dimension is a world in which the flow of light can be sensed.

5. Sensing Love

Another characteristic of the fifth dimension is the awakening of a new level of love. Here on Earth, we experience many kinds of love: romantic love, love between parents and children, love between friends, and love between masters and pupils. But the love experienced by the inhabitants of the fifth dimension is much purer. On Earth, love is often difficult to express and communicate, but this is not the case in the World of Goodness. When you have feelings of love towards someone in the fifth dimension, that person feels those vibrations directly, and the love that is communicated becomes the soul's experiences of joy. Because love cannot be felt so clearly on Earth, people can never be completely sure if they are loved. This leads to a lot of suffering. It also makes romantic love here on Earth particularly complicated, like a tightrope we are forced to walk in the hope that we will be met on the other side.

In the fifth dimension, however, we are never in doubt about the presence of love. All souls can sense love instantly, including variations in the strength of love they are receiving; it is as if love's energy is flowing through them. Their heart starts to feel very warm, and they begin to feel very happy. They can *feel* the love the way we can see the difference between the light of fluorescent and incandescent light bulbs, or between sixty-watt and one hundred- or two hundred-watt light bulbs.

So far, I have only been referring to love, but all thoughts and emotions in the World of Goodness, or the fifth dimension, are transmitted instantly and directly. This is why the inhabitants of Hell cannot be permitted to dwell here: such spirits are full of hatred, envy, dissatisfaction, anger, and insatiable desire, and if these emotions were to be broadcast everywhere, the fifth dimension of Heaven would cease to exist.

Though there are variations in strength and level, all souls of the fifth dimension have love, and they are all power generators who supply love. After they have gained a certain amount of experience expressing and receiving love, spirits in this dimension are visited by higher beings from the sixth dimension. Just as angels go down to the fourth dimension to offer guidance about life after the loss of the physical body, beings from the sixth dimension provide further insights into the nature of love, including reminders that the deepest love comes from the mind of God.

Souls who live in the fifth dimension can sense the workings of God on a basic level, but they are still striving to achieve a clear understanding of who God is. The higher spirits teach them by pointing to the Spiritual Sun floating in the sky and showing them that this is the highest form of love. The Spiritual Sun provides everyone in the fifth dimension with warmth and energy without ever asking anything in return, so it is a pure expression of unconditional love and compassion. The higher spirits teach souls in the fifth dimension that as children of God, our true essence is a part of His very being. The joy that overwhelms us when we share vibrations of love with another person or spirit is proof of this larger Truth.

This is a very basic level of our education on love, which truly begins in the fifth dimension. It does not reach as far as learning to give love to others, which is practiced in the World of Bodhisattvas in the seventh dimension, but it does instruct spirits in the fundamentals: what love is and what it is to love and be loved. Those living in the fifth dimension learn that it is better to be loved than not, and what a wonderful thing it is to love others. Eventually, they gain the fuller understanding that love truly cannot coexist with a desire for self-preservation or with a feeling that one's own well-being is all that matters.

6. *The Purpose of Sorrow and Pain*

Throughout history, people have looked to Heaven as an eternal paradise where pain and sorrow are unknown. But is this really true? Is it true that such feelings disappear completely in the worlds beyond Hell, in the fourth and fifth dimensions? Do people in Heaven do nothing but smile and laugh? Are tears and sorrow things that God neither intended nor created?

No one can deny that joy and anger, sorrow and pleasure are the most basic emotions we experience as human beings. But do they truly exist in and of themselves? There has been a lot of debate on this point between supporters of the philosophies of monism and dualism. The monist movement defines evil as the absence of good and cold as the absence of heat. Ralph Waldo Emerson pioneered this philosophical movement. While this philosophy has some merit, it also has significant limitations. It is certainly true that cold requires the absence of heat and that evil exists in the absence of good, but there is more to it than that. We don't cry whenever we do not feel happy, we cry specifically because we are sad, so sadness must be an emotion in and of itself.

Another example is pain, which is more than just the absence of pleasure. Pain has an existence all its own. Pain and pleasure are certainly connected. For example, when you engage in a physically demanding sport such as long-distance running, at first you may feel fatigue and exhaustion, but once you cross a certain pain threshold, those feelings give way to a sense of exhilaration. However, it is an undeniable fact that you first experience a type of pain.

Thus, it is very clear that both this world and the next have a dualistic nature. Basic emotions such as joy, anger, sorrow, and pleasure do not just exist in the absence of their opposites, but in addition to their opposites. God is an exception to this rule, however. His being is good, and only good; he is all light and love. But there was a reason why He created the third dimension that we live in and the lower levels of the spirit world, the fourth and fifth dimensions. He formed them because He wished to create a system that would foster the development of our souls.

It is very difficult for our souls to grow without opportunities to refine themselves through adversity and through experience in a world of relativity. A world that contains only happiness might seem like a wonderful place, but how could we ever experience the even more profound joys of spiritual growth and of helping others? This would be impossible because none of those happy people would have any need of assistance or feel the need for improvement! This is why God saw to it that sad or painful experiences would be part of the three-dimensional world on Earth and the lower worlds of the spirit world; they facilitate the progress of our souls.

Some spirits in the fifth dimension have difficulty actualizing their dreams and goals (even though they are far more likely to do so than we are). Like us in this world, they pray, but whether their wishes are answered or not depends on the person. From the perspective of spirits residing in the higher dimensions, some of their prayers are premature, and will require time before they can be granted. So when these prayers are not fulfilled, spirits in the fifth dimension experience sadness and pain. This gives them opportunities to refine and develop themselves into souls with even greater resilience and strength.

7. Sorrow and Pain Are Nourishment for Our Souls

Thus, although some schools of thought contend that all suffering and pain are only delusions and do not exist in and of themselves, this is not the truth. It is true that the Primordial God, is perfect, and therefore lacks nothing. No growth, no progress, is necessary for Him. He is the greatest love and the greatest happiness, and therefore, the ultimate good, the ultimate truth, and the ultimate beauty. Because He already embodies these characteristics, He can make no progress in them, nor can He experience the joy of developing them further. Nor does He need them. But in His infinite wisdom, He has made such development possible for us.

The Primordial God created the great universe as if He were a landscape architect. He placed a rock here; formed a pond there and stocked it with fish; planted trees of varying types and sizes, including some that bear fruit; and even planted weeds. What might appear as an imperfection to us was something that the Primordial God created intentionally to give His garden the ambience He desired. He thought it would be nice to have a few weeds. He took pleasure in providing rich variety, creating mountains, hills, and promontories as well as valleys and low-lying swamps. Everything in the universe was created according to His intentions, and its miraculous diversity is a sign that the Primordial God is enjoying His job.

Pain and sorrow are permitted to exist in the third, fourth, and fifth dimensions under certain conditions not because they are "good by nature" but because they provide us with chances to make great leaps forward in our personal and spiritual growth. When you wish to accomplish or experience something, but it doesn't happen, you feel pain and sorrow that doesn't quite go away. And when our efforts result in something quite different from what we hoped for, this too can lead to feelings of painful disappointment or tearful sadness. But the Primordial God, the architect of our experience, is not allowing these tears to exist for their own sake; our sweat and toil and disappointment are only intended to provide us with a way to reach a higher level.

Our struggles can lead us to a feeling of exhilaration, much like they do for the long-distance runner. Therefore, we must not look upon this world as a tragic place, full of pain and sorrow. Rather, we should accept the fact that pain and sorrow exist, but recognize that their role is to act as whetstones that help us polish our souls into something better and more beautiful. We are diamonds in the rough, and we attain our luster by meeting with resistance from abrasion. Without such resistance, we would have no way to develop the brilliant shine that sets us apart from other stones.

In much the same way, sorrow and pain have been created for our growth, but they are not intended to last forever. They are only fleeting experiences that have been provided as a way to nourish the soul. We are all meant to eventually travel on to a world of joy and delight, a world of everlasting happiness, an endless paradise.

8. Discovering Your Divine Light

Pain and sorrow may exist for the development of our souls, but how does this help us get through those terrible times when we seem to be overwhelmed by hardship? William

Shakespeare, one of the greatest playwrights in history, wrote numerous tragedies. He penned them to show the world that there is light at the heart of every misfortune. We often think that light comes only from above, but this is only part of the truth. He wanted people to know that when we are in the depths of despair and believe that things could get no worse, the floor can open up beneath us and immerse us in light. By falling through the bottom of tragedy, we discover a Truth of our humanity and the shining light hidden within our being. Comedies, plays with happy endings (which Shakespeare also wrote), are not the only way to encourage people to grow and progress, and in fact, things that appear to be tragic could very well be shortcuts to the light.

There are many people in this world who curse their fate, wondering, "Why am I always the one to suffer? Why do I have such bad luck?" They may have lost their parents in childhood, or they may not have been able to afford to go to school, or they may not have ever been married. If they did marry, they may have been separated from their beloved by death or by choice. Perhaps they could not have any children, or their children died young. Perhaps their children became addicts, or turned their backs on their families. There is no end to the reasons why people suffer; the seeds of sorrow are without number.

But this is not to say that these experiences of sorrow, tragedy, and what seems to be bad luck are meaningless, or have no use to us. The world where we resided before we were born on Earth, called Heaven, is a place with very little of this pain and sorrow. In this world in the third dimension, however, unlike in Heaven, active forms of evil do exist, and torrents of ill fortune can bear down on us and make it seem as though we are completely at the mercy of fate. But we should not forget the Biblical story of Job, who experienced so many adversities and misfortunes that in his despair he cursed God. God replied, "Are you so wise that you can judge the Will of God? Be more humble. Do you really understand my intentions?"

God was really saying to Job, "The obstacles you face are just stage props that I have created for the purpose of helping humans evolve." People who have passed away, leaving us behind in this world, may now be living marvelous lives in the next world. This tells us that we must not judge things from the limited perspective of this world. What looks to be misfortune is actually for the best, even if you don't know it yet. The more trials you face, the closer you are to the light. In the midst of joy, Heaven is near, but you are also approaching Heaven when you find yourself in the depths of sorrow. I hope that many people will discover this Truth. Find the courage to burst through the floor of the darkest pit of sorrow and reach for the light that is within you, and don't let go of the light that streams up from below; then Heaven will surely appear before you.

9. True Nobility

"Nobility" is a word that refers to integrity, excellence, and greatness. Someone of noble character possesses great and valuable virtues. So who are these noble souls? Let's consider a man who is the first-born son of a rich family, living in a large mansion complete with servants. Looking back on his childhood, he remembers his every need being fulfilled. Intelligent, popular, and very good-looking, this man moved easily in the highest social circles, and his many business ventures prospered. He married, had children, lived a full life, and eventually died, mourned by friends and family alike. Is he an example of the nobility of the soul? Is he someone we might call a great man?

I believe not. People whose souls are imbued with nobility are known for their selflessness and their high moral character, and such virtues can only be found in those who have braved great trials, overcome them, and gone on to make a difference in other people's lives. Isn't overcoming adversity how such people develop and demonstrate the nobility of their character?

Think of Dr. Albert Schweitzer, a Divine Spirit who prevailed over the hardships of life in the remote jungles of Africa to spread the word of God and provide medical care for suffering indigenous people. Thomas Edison had only a limited formal education but went on to become one of the greatest inventors the world has ever known. Abraham Lincoln was born to a poor family, but through tireless perseverance, he educated himself, became a lawyer, entered politics, became president of the United States, and guided his nation to unity after a devastating civil war. Mohandas K. Gandhi used nonviolent tactics to confront the military might of the British Empire and won independence for his country.

When we look at the lives of any one of these remarkable Divine Spirits, we can see that suffering and hardship are not just impediments to be overcome, but provide the very means by which we give beauty, meaning, and nobility to our time on Earth. This is the true purpose of suffering and hardship.

Of course, this is not just true of life in modern times; it has been true throughout history. Shakyamuni Buddha, the founder of Buddhism, was born a prince and surrounded by everything he could possibly desire. But one day he decided to cast all that away, and at age twenty-nine, he left his family and the comforts of the palace behind to set out on a journey to enlightenment. When we make a decision to take a stand against all odds for the sake of achieving a greater purpose, the nobility of our souls begins to shine. This greatness will in turn serve as a beacon for future generations. I am always filled with encouragement whenever I look at the history of humankind and discover countless men and women of great virtue and high resolve, whose noble spirits sparkle like a river of stars in the galaxy.

There is no telling when we ourselves may be faced with hardship and adversity in the course of our own lives. History is filled with people too numerous to mention who were confronted with terrible difficulties. Those who were crushed by these trials were forgotten over time, but those who found the means to withstand and overcome their misfortunes were able to realize the nobility of their souls, which became their immortal medals of honorable achievement. If the life of Jesus had been overwhelmed by hardship, his name would have been lost to the passage of time. He became a beacon of glorious light for the world because he exercised his greatness by persevering in times of adversity.

10. *Moments of Spiritual Guidance*

People who live in fortunate circumstances should be grateful for their blessings. They should also work hard to improve themselves, both for their own personal development and for the greater well-being of others. People who are blessed by good fortune or who are especially gifted or talented have a moral obligation to develop their gifts fully and push themselves to achieve even higher goals.

On the other hand, if you live in poverty, or seem to

lack talent, or live with a physical handicap or chronic illness, these hardships can contain a hidden blessing. These obstacles provide opportunities to find ways to propel your soul towards achieving something better. By seizing these opportunities, you can grow and evolve. Remember that there is very little to be gained from lamenting your misfortune. But by living with your difficult circumstances, by carrying this cross with dignity, you nourish your soul. If you live your life with dignity, a light will begin to shine from within you.

Of course, you should not go out of your way to inflict adversity on yourself. There is no need for you to actively seek hardships and difficulties. Instead, strive to develop a dauntless spirit that will give you the strength to overcome any hardships, should they befall you. Rather than being disappointed about what you do not have, discover the splendor of what you have been given, and use it as your tool. Those who are blind may be able to speak most eloquently, and those who cannot walk may have hands that are unusually dexterous. Those who are especially intelligent may not be athletic, and vice versa. Rather than comparing yourself with others and being disappointed by what you do not have, turn your eyes to those things you have been blessed with, your strengths, and exert all the power you have to take them as far as they can go. In working to expand your strengths, you will surely find clues to completing the set of assignments that have been given to you in this lifetime. Everyone's life is filled with mysteries to solve, obstacles to surmount, and challenging missions to fulfill; life is a workbook with a series of assignments we were given to complete, and somewhere within its very pages, there is always a clue that will help us on our way.

If you were to examine yourself through another person's eyes, you would find that you are superior to other people in some ways, and inferior in others. If you discover ways in which you excel or fall short compared to others, think of them as the clues to completing your life's workbook. Next, it is important to repeatedly ask yourself why you were given these particular assignments; the answer to this question describes one of the primary objectives of your spiritual training in this life.

People face all kinds of limitations, from physical to mental, and your purpose and mission in this incarnation are to be found within your limitations, too. When you discover what your assignments are, you have actually been spiritually guided. When you become aware of your weaknesses and determine to courageously fight against them, the necessary courage will surely rise. It is in these moments that Divine Spirits in the other world, including your own guardian spirit and Guiding Spirit, will send you great strength. Therefore, continually search for the clues that are hidden in your life's workbook. When you make an all-out effort to use these clues to complete your assignments, you will be provided with the boundless support of the Divine Spirits.

When we become aware that the essence of the soul is its desire to grow, we come to the realization that it is our task, as humans, to give total effort on the soul's behalf. Indeed, our souls were given eternal life so that we may pursue infinite growth; every one of the assignments we complete and the problems we solve becomes valuable nourishment that fosters our soul's growth. Completing our challenging assignments gives us nobility and adds more brilliance to our inner light. It is my hope that you will be able to surmount the problems that have been assigned to you, and I pray that you will recognize and seize upon many of the clues to finding solutions, for these are signs of precious spiritual guidance.

3

THE WORLD
OF THE
SIXTH DIMENSION

1. A World of Divine Spirits

In this chapter, I would like to describe various aspects of life in the sixth dimension, also known as the World of Light. In the previous chapters, we considered the fourth and fifth dimensions, to which people usually return not long after death. When souls reach the sixth dimension, they are truly entering the world of the Divine Spirits. Since ancient times, the afterworld has been known as home to the gods, and indeed this description could well apply to the World of Light. But what kinds of gods live here?

It is important to note that God the Creator, who produced the universe, does not reside in the World of Light. The gods we are referring to are spirits who were extremely virtuous and who achieved extraordinary things during their incarnate time on Earth. Because of their exceptional accomplishments and elevated souls, people did not consider them to be ordinary human beings, but believed they were more like gods. One example is the famous Japanese scholar and politician Sugawara-no-Michizane, who lived in the ninth century. Soon after he died, people began worshiping him as the god of learning.

On the whole, people who return to the world of the sixth dimension are those who have contributed to society while on Earth, who have earned the respect of others, and whose hearts are not attuned to Hell. These people are much more spiritually evolved than the average person. On Earth, their extraordinary abilities often inspire awe, which contributes to people's tendency to worship them. Many Japanese gods in the pantheon of the Shinto religion also reside in the sixth dimension.

2. *The Definition of Divine Spirits*

We still haven't defined exactly what we mean by the word *God*. This is an issue that has long been debated by students and teachers of philosophy, religion, and theology. Some have declared, "To know God is to know everything," while others have boldly stated, "Human beings were not made in the image of God; rather, God is a figment of the imagination created in the image of man." However, to my way of thinking, no one has ever offered a clear and precise answer to the question, who or what is God? In an attempt to fill that void, I would like to offer my thoughts on the matter.

First, we need to differentiate between God the Creator and all lesser gods. Christianity preaches the doctrine of the Holy Trinity—the Father, the Son, and the Holy Spirit. Some see only the Father as God, but all three dimensions are essential to the entity that Christians identify as God. The word *god* refers to an entity that is spiritually superior to human beings. So in that broad, nondenominational sense, the Holy Spirit could be called a god of the kind that we find in the sixth dimension, along with gods of the Shinto religion. But God the Creator exists in a much higher dimension.

Not all the inhabitants of the sixth dimension are gods, however. The World of Light contains a number of different levels. You may imagine transparent barriers dividing the sixth dimension into different neighborhoods, where spirits live according to their spiritual advancement, as if living on different floors in a high-rise apartment building. However, these inhabitants of the sixth dimension no longer have bodies. Now they live as a conscious form of energy, which still has specific characteristics and therefore individuality. When I say that there are different levels within the sixth dimension, I'm referring to differences in the wavelengths, or vibrations, of the spirits that reside there. The result is a natural division into groups of spirits with different wave-lengths.

To envision this in a way that might be easier to understand, imagine filling a cup with muddy water. If you let it sit for a while, the heavier particles will sink to the bottom and the water at the top of the cup will gradually become clear. The nearer you are to the top of the glass, the clearer the water will be. In the same way, conscious spiritual entities that are still weighted down by materialistic values sink to the lower part of the sixth dimension. Purer consciousnesses, or spirits that have less attachment to this earthly world, rise to the upper part, closer to God the Creator. Spirits reside in a given region of the World of Light according to their spiritual nature.

COMMUNICATION
IN THE SPIRIT WORLD

•

In the spirit world, space spreads out in all directions, but there is no physical distance. Even though people may appear to be tens or hundreds of kilometers apart, if their hearts are close to each other—that is to say, if they have the same spiritual vibrations—then they can communicate with each other instantly. It is like looking at a television: as soon as we turn on the switch, the image appears. On television, we can see events that take place on the other side of the globe almost instantaneously. Similarly, in the spirit world, spirits can communicate with each other instantly by tuning into the right channel, or the same spiritual vibrations.

On the other hand, people whose hearts remain distant from each other will feel like they are far away even if they are physically very close. Even if they are in the same space, they might pass each other without noticing. If their hearts are facing in different directions, or they have completely different spiritual vibrations, they become invisible to each other.

Another electric device that shows how communication works in the spirit world is the telephone. By using the telephone, we can talk to someone hundreds of kilometers away. Spirits can communicate with each other in the spirit world very much as if they were on the telephone, and when they are connected, they become very close to each other. In this way, the spirit world works very much like a telephone or television.

3. Seeking Enlightenment

The first step towards enlightenment is learning that the
world beyond this one is populated by conscious forms of
energy that rise to different dimensions depending on their
degree of awareness. There are also different levels of enlightenment. At a lower level, attaining enlightenment means
truly accepting that human beings are more than their physical bodies. Simple as it may seem, this key understanding is
definitely a form of enlightenment. Only a small percentage
of the spirits in the fourth dimension have reached this level
of awareness; many of them do not know that they are essentially souls, and that they no longer have physical bodies.

Another kind of enlightenment is the one that spirits
need if they are to rise from Hell to Heaven. While they
are in Hell, spirits care nothing for others; they live only
to fulfill their selfish desires, and can't understand what is
wrong with that approach. However, after living in Hell with
like-minded people for years, decades, or even centuries, they
eventually become disgusted with their surroundings and
begin to change their attitude. This form of enlightenment
is the first step in the transition from Hell to Heaven. When
they finally see the error of their ways and understand that
there is more to life than self-preservation, they return to
the Astral Realm, the upper part of the fourth dimension.

Their next step is to fully accept the importance of goodness, which allows them to ascend to the fifth dimension, the World of Goodness.

The sixth dimension is reserved for those who are serious about seeking enlightenment, those who have turned their full awareness towards the Divine. You will find no atheists in the sixth dimension. By this stage all spirits realize, to a greater or lesser extent, that some kind of great spiritual being is responsible for everything in Creation. Some people may call this entity God, and others Buddha, but these are just different names for the same Creator. The paths these spirits take also vary, but they all walk towards this Supreme Existence.

Numerous priests, monks, and spiritual teachers of different religions who devote themselves to studying the issue of divinity live in the sixth dimension, although having been a spiritual devotee is not a requirement for dwelling in the World of Light. Some residents might not have wholeheartedly pursued God or Buddha, but found other ways to attain a high level of spiritual development through their professions on Earth. For example, a great number of scholars reside in the sixth dimension—university professors and teachers who devoted themselves to the advancement of academic knowledge while keeping their hearts attuned to Heaven. You will also find doctors, lawyers, and judges, as well as politicians and government officials who were able to retain pure hearts.

Artists and musicians who cultivated their artistic talents and evolved spiritually also live in the sixth dimension. On the whole, spirits in the sixth dimension contributed to spiritual progress in whatever they did on Earth.

The primary job of spirits in the sixth dimension is to provide inspiration to people on Earth. They do this in ways that accord with the professions they pursued when they lived in the material world. Those who were monks, priests, or ministers offer religious guidance to people on Earth. Those who were active in politics offer advice to politicians in this world. Those who were government officials guide people who work in government offices, those who were artists send inspiration to artists, and those who used to be college professors guide those who are studying on Earth. Providing inspiration to the people in their field of specialization moves these spirits closer to enlightenment. By guiding people on Earth, they are preparing to move on to the next stage—to enter the world of the seventh dimension—by experiencing what it is like to work for the sake of others.

In sum, the quality that the spirits in the sixth dimension share is usefulness—the ability to contribute to the spiritual development and advancement of the world. This quality is still at too early a stage to be described as true love, but it prepares the way for true love.

4. An Ocean of Light

A more detailed description of the sixth dimension may help you imagine it more vividly. For one thing, the higher a dimension is, the brighter its light, which means that when you arrive in the World of Light of the sixth dimension, it is really quite dazzling. You may have had the experience of driving through the mountains and suddenly coming to a spectacular panoramic view of high, craggy peaks, or of a town down in a distant valley, or of steep cliffs plunging headlong to the sea. The sudden change of scenery takes your breath away, which is exactly what people experience when they enter the sixth dimension for the first time. Like the sea reflecting the strong sunshine of summer, at first the sixth dimension is too bright to look at directly; it takes some time to adjust to the sight. This world is indeed an ocean of light. This sea I mention is not just an analogy, for an extremely beautiful sea does indeed exist in the World of Light of the sixth dimension.

As I stated earlier, the sixth dimension contains a number of different realms that exist on different levels. The sixth dimension is also divided horizontally. On the front side is Major Heaven, the World of Light of the sixth dimension that we've already discussed. Major Heaven is reserved for those Divine Spirits whose efforts developed and improved their souls during their time on Earth. On the back side of Heaven, also known as Minor Heaven, different kinds of spirits reside in various realms. One of these is the Realm of Sea Gods, a vast world set within a sea of light often described in Japanese folk tales and legends as the home of the sea gods. Many Divine Spirits reside in this realm. Although the Realm of Sea Gods belongs mostly to the sixth dimension, it also floats across the fourth and fifth dimensions.

All kinds of creatures live in the Realm of Sea Gods, including dragon gods. These dragon gods are not human spirits, but they serve as emissaries of the Divine Spirits in the Realm of Sea Gods. Dragon gods possess tremendous spiritual power. They have the ability to cause natural phenomena on Earth, and they have generated tremendous amounts of energy at major turning points in history.

Other realms of the sixth dimension in Minor Heaven include the Sennin (hermit wizards) Realm and the Tengu (long-nosed wizards) Realm. While the Realm of Sea Gods is oceanic, the Sennin Realm and the Tengu Realm are mountainous. The various types of spirits living in these realms are engaged in ascetic discipline as a way of attaining supernatural powers and achieving enlightenment. The people who return to these realms are those who tried to gain psychic powers by concentrating on physical disciplines during their life on Earth. Because these spirits now focus exclusively on metaphysical forces, they tend to lack human warmth and kindness.

5. Eternal Travelers

Humans are essentially eternal travelers on the path of spiritual evolution. Some may question why we have to continually strive for spiritual development if we feel that there is nothing wrong with the way we are now. On one level, they have a point. But it is also true that if we stayed the way we are for all eternity, our souls would stagnate. Our souls are eternal, and we will continue to exist not just for thousands or millions of years, but for billions of years and more. If we did not improve, our souls would not experience the joy that comes from spiritual development. In other words, we would become bored. It may be fine to do the same thing for a few hundred years, but at some point, our souls begin to want something more. The soul is intended to be productive and creative. This is its true nature.

As long as we have a personality and individual consciousness, we feel we have to achieve something. Take the example of office workers, many of whom dream of leaving their company one day and spending their time doing whatever they want to do. However, when they finally retire from their company and become free to pursue whatever they like, they don't know what to do with themselves. They may be free, but most of them cannot bear being unproductive, and within a year or two, they start looking for another job or devote themselves to a hobby. It is the essential nature of our souls to be industrious rather than inactive.

Although everyone may slack off now and then, we cannot bear to vegetate for long periods of time. Human beings have a natural desire to work. We should therefore constantly strive to do the best possible job at whatever we do, especially spiritual undertakings, so that our souls can experience contentment, peace, and happiness. This diligent nature reflects the Truth that human souls are eternal travelers walking on the path of spiritual evolution.

6. Polishing Our Diamonds Within

When you hear that we human beings seek the evolution of the soul, you may ask, "Why? Why should there be different levels in the spirit world? Why should there be superior and inferior spirits? Why should there be Guiding Spirits of Light and ordinary spirits? If God loves everyone equally, why should there be differences?" My answer is that all people are created like diamonds that will gleam brilliantly if they are cut and polished, but when diamonds are first dug out of the mountain, they are still in a rough state. We all have the same essence, but it is up to the individual how much we shine. This is a responsibility that no one can avoid.

When you think about the difference between Guiding Spirits of Light and ordinary spirits, you may agree that Guiding Spirits of Light are like diamonds, but you may feel that ordinary spirits are like stones by the riverbank that will never achieve the beauty of diamonds. But this is not true. Every soul is a diamond inside, no matter how rough its exterior may be. And every stone, or soul, will shine if it is polished.

This is true of spirits in Hell, too. When people on Earth hear stories about devils and the spirits of Hell, they often wonder why such beings are allowed to exist at all. Why doesn't God drive them out of the spirit world altogether, even out of Hell, and banish them to some distant corner of the galaxy? However human this feeling may be, it is based on a lack of awareness of the true nature of the soul. You may think that the spirits of Hell will never stop harming others, but this is not necessarily the case. Given the chance, they can straighten themselves out and start heading down the right path.

I have had many occasions to meet with people who were possessed by evil spirits, and I have spoken directly to those spirits. When I did, I realized that they were simply unaware of their true nature. The spirits in Hell do not know that human beings are more than just their physical bodies. They are not even aware of the fact that they are presently living in Hell, much less that they are supposed to do good for the benefit of others. The spirits of Hell are not evil in and of themselves; they are just ignorant.

This means that when we teach them God's Truths, and when they realize that they have been living a false life, they can change. They can make the decision to live properly. And the moment they do, their dark spiritual bodies begin to radiate light: a halo appears behind their head. Why would their bodies shine if not as proof that even malicious spirits, even devils, are diamonds at heart? They may look like ordinary stones, which might tempt you to throw them away, but if you cut and polish them, they will shine as brilliantly as any star. In this sense, we all have infinite potential. And this infinite potential that we have been given is another expression of God's boundless love for us.

7. The Nature of Leadership

The world is full of people who wish to attain worldly success, and many aspire to positions of power as well. Some seek to become president, or a member of the cabinet, or some other high office. Ironically, at the same time that such people seek respect and power, they can be quick to ridicule politicians, perhaps because they are disgusted by the naked ambition and arrogance that we have come to associate with politics.

Today, too many people have lost sight of the true nature of politics, which is basically a form of hierarchy based on an agreement between the ruler and the ruled. It resembles a pyramid in which a few people stand at the top, supported by a large number of people at the base. Because of its triangular shape, this is a very stable structure. If it were circular, for example, and there were no hierarchy, it would be far too unsteady.

The vast majority of corporations also have a pyramidal structure: most employees are found at the base, and as you rise, the number of people gets smaller and smaller. At the very pinnacle of management, you find one person, the CEO. Even schools have this same structure, with the principal at the top, followed by an assistant principal, and many teachers below them. In universities, there are professors and deans, and the president at the very top.

This pyramid is actually a reflection of the structure of the spirit world. There are more people in the fourth dimension than in the fifth, more in the fifth than in the sixth, and so on until one arrives at the ninth dimension where only ten Grand Spirits reside. Just as leaders in the spirit world guide other spirits, we need people on Earth who will guide other people. We need leaders to unify people with different opinions and lead the community; this idea lies at the foundation of politics. Spirits in the World of Light of the sixth dimension are striving to improve their abilities as leaders. On Earth they may have been involved in a wide variety of professions, but what they all have in common is the potential to become great leaders.

8. Drawing Power from God

Having said that spirits in the sixth dimension are meant to take on the mantle of leadership, I would like to pose the question, why? Why should they have the power to make others follow their orders? What gives them the right to instruct other spirits? What is the basis of their political authority, or more specifically, their spiritual power? The answer is that spiritual power is bestowed from above. In other words, it originates with God.

God is like the North Star, constantly showing us the right direction to travel. By walking toward God, we can judge what is right and wrong—which direction will lead us to Hell and which to Heaven. Those who stand close to God instruct those below. The many leaders in the sixth dimension derive their power from the power and wisdom that flow to them from God. Without this power, the spirits in the World of Light would be incapable of helping anyone, either on Earth or in the spirit world. It is only when we know that our ideas are supported by God that we can become truly valiant and emit light.

Spirits in the sixth dimension know that they have been chosen by God and that they are among the true elite, so they feel an obligation to guide those in lower dimensions, who are less developed. Although their teaching methods may differ, all the Divine Spirits in the sixth dimension devote themselves to studying and conveying the Will of God in the way that best suits their capabilities.

These spirits have overwhelming power to guide others. They can say with confidence, "From what I have learned, this is God's Will, which is why we should adopt the following policies." To put it simply, knowing God's Will is their primary objective, and it is also the source of their authority. To know God's Will, one must study God's Truths. The prerequisite for entering the sixth dimension is an eagerness to acquire the knowledge of the Truths. The requirement for staying in the sixth dimension is to gain that wisdom.

9. The Power of God's Words

There is a famous quote from the Christian Bible that reads: "In the beginning was the Word, and the Word was with God, and the Word was God" (John I:I) When the Guiding Spirits of Light are born on Earth, it is their words that persuade and inspire others. Of course, they sometimes perform miracles, but these supernatural phenomena alone are not sufficient; while they can be useful in attracting people's attention, they do not in themselves lead others to true awakening. They must be accompanied by words.

Have you ever wondered why words have such amazing power? Why is it that we can be so moved when we hear someone speak? When the Guiding Spirits of Light preach or give lectures, why do their words have the power to touch our hearts? Why do they move us to tears?

We are so deeply touched when we hear someone speak the Truths in this world because deep in our hearts, we remember having heard the Truths before. Our souls remember when we heard the Truths preached on Earth by different Guiding Spirits of Light, such as Shakyamuni Buddha in India, or Jesus Christ in Palestine. We also resonate with memories of hearing the Guiding Spirits of Light teach us the Truths in the other world, in the fourth dimension and above. When words evoke these deep memories within our souls, they stir profound emotions.

We do not cry only when we are sad; we also shed tears of joy. The tears we weep upon encountering God's Truths, or the words of the enlightened ones, are known as "the rain of God's words." These tears have the power to cleanse our hearts, and to purify us by removing worldly desires. Just as rain from the sky washes dust out of the air, so the rain of

God's words washes away our sins. As we shed these tears, our hearts begin to shine like beacons of light.

Religious leaders on Earth need to provide as many opportunities as possible to bring forth the rain of God's words. Conveying powerful words in writing is important, but even more important is conveying them aloud through speaking. By giving lectures to large numbers of people and talking to people one on one, spiritual leaders can inspire people and move them to tears. When people are moved, they reawaken their memories of their spirituality and feel a strong desire to enter the path to enlightenment.

When you read the writings of an enlightened person, you can feel his or her passion and be inspired by it. The lectures and writings of a spiritually undeveloped person don't have this effect because words have power according to their speaker's level of enlightenment, or the depth of his or her understanding of the Truths. The higher the level of your enlightenment becomes, the more power your words have to touch the hearts of others.

If you would like to test your own level of enlightenment, give a talk based on your knowledge of the Truths—for example, that human beings are more than just their physical bodies—and see if your words have the power to inspire people. The higher the level of your enlightenment, the more powerful your words become, and when your words are filled with light, they will never fail to touch the hearts of others.

This is a very useful way to check how much progress you have made in your spiritual training.

10. *Towards the World of Love*

As we have seen in this chapter, the spirit world of the sixth dimension is divided into upper, middle, and lower levels, and is also divided horizontally. The World of Light exists in the front, the Realm of Sea Gods in the middle, and in the back of the sixth dimension we have the Tengu Realm and the Sennin Realm, where spirits devote themselves to ascetic discipline. Those who like to show off their power return to the Tengu Realm, while the Sennin Realm is for those focusing on perfecting supernatural powers.

As I mentioned earlier, numerous spirits who are worshipped as gods reside in the sixth dimension, primarily in the upper part of the World of Light. Among them are Buddhist deities such as Vaisravana, the god of wealth, and many gods of Shintoism, including the god of fortune. Given the high level of these spirits, they do not necessarily belong to the sixth dimension. Some of them have attained the enlightenment of the seventh or eighth dimension, but choose to be in the upper part of the sixth dimension to carry out a particular mission. In other words, these god-like spirits often possess a higher level of enlightenment than required for the sixth dimension. There are many cases where tathagatas (who reside in the eighth dimension) and bodhisattvas (who reside in the seventh dimension) come down to the sixth dimension to supervise and to train spirits in the best ways to guide people on Earth. These are the Divine Spirits that are worshipped as gods on Earth.

Another group of spirits in the upper part of the sixth dimension are known in Buddhism as arhats, those who are pursuing a spiritual discipline in order to attain the state of bodhisattvas in the seventh dimension. These arhats have purified their hearts and minds, have corrected their mistakes through self-reflection, and have halos above their heads. Although they have taken the first step up the ladder to the seventh dimension, arhats still live in the upper part of the World of Light. Although arhat is a Buddhist term, some Christians and people of other faiths have also attained the state of arhat and reside here.

To become an arhat, you have to have attained a certain level of personal discipline. Arhats constantly strive to improve themselves in an effort to enter the world of the seventh dimension. They work to acquire knowledge of God's Truths while exploring ways to teach others what they have learned. The prerequisite for advancing to the next level is attaining a state of mind in which you are filled with love and compassion and live for the sake of helping others. When arhats attain this state of mind, they become bodhisattvas, or angels.

One of the primary objectives of the training in the World of Light is to prepare spirits to become bodhisattvas. But before beginning this training, spirits need to distinguish themselves in a certain field so that it is clear that they have the expertise necessary to help others. Unless they complete the required disciplines in the sixth dimension, they cannot advance to the seventh dimension. The same is true of spiritual training in this world, on Earth. Things must happen in the proper order. We cannot devote ourselves to giving love until we first acquire knowledge of the Truths and put them into practice. The first step is to gain a firm understanding of the Truths. Next, in a spirit of unconditional love, we use our knowledge and experience to help others: we save them through the power of enlightenment. This is the right path to follow, and it is consistent with the structure of the spirit world.

4

THE WORLD
OF THE
SEVENTH DIMENSION

1. A World of Love

In this chapter, I would like to explore the domain of souls in the seventh dimension, which also goes by the Buddhist name of the World of Bodhisattvas. If the seventh dimension were to be described succinctly, it could be summed up as "a world of love." Of course, love means many things to many people, and perhaps it is this fluid, protean quality that has made it the enduring subject of music, art, poetry, novels, philosophical texts, and all kinds of creative endeavors.

Despite all this creative output, no one in all of history has provided a conclusive definition of love, a definition beyond debate that describes love's true essence. Still, we can all agree that our need for love is one of the most basic qualities of being human, and love is something we go to almost any lengths to attain. Everyone wants to be loved, and how we manage the disparity between our *desire to be loved* and the feeling of actually *being loved* plays a crucial role in whether or not we are happy. For this reason, I would like to inquire more deeply into the nature of love, and make it the focus of this chapter.

In the previous chapter, I mentioned that knowledge is very important in the sixth dimension—not merely an accumulation of earthly knowledge, but the knowledge of God's Truths. One dimension above this world of knowledge lies the world of love. Love surpasses knowledge, but just as the sixth dimension is a prerequisite for the seventh, knowledge of God's Truths is the basis for the highest form of love. So while knowledge is important, love transcends it. We can find evidence for this insight in our own experience.

Love appears to be a simple thing to practice, but in truth it is very difficult. This is because one of the basic aspects of love is nurturing people and encouraging them to grow as human beings. To foster other people's progress, you need to have a deep understanding of people, the world, the true nature of people's hearts and minds, and the Will of God. All these are difficult to grasp. This is why love based on a true foundation of knowledge can do real good in the world, while love not grounded in knowledge is fragile and delicate, and all too quickly withers and dies. We see an example of this frail form of love in people who perform many charitable works but are still unhappy because their good deeds don't elicit the gratitude they expect. They are doing the right things for the wrong reasons, or in a wrong way. If their love were grounded in wisdom or an understanding of others, they would know exactly what to do to make people truly happy. Their charitable work would be a gift of love, and would be received with gratitude.

This comparison of two types of love leads us to a crucial truth about love. If we delve deeply into the true essence of our minds, we will see that there is a form of love that pours out like water from an endless underground spring. It gushes from the innermost part of our being and never dries out. This insight is a good starting point for advancing our understanding of love throughout this chapter.

2. The Beginnings of Love

What role does love play in our lives? How does it serve us? Is it something that always existed from the very beginning, or did humans feel a need and invent love to fill it? What would happen if love disappeared? These are some of the questions I would like to try to answer in this section.

Life lasts quite a long time; most of us will live as long as sixty or seventy years. There must be a life-sustaining force that continuously spurs us forward, that carries us through the many decades we live on Earth. This will be the first subject of our contemplation.

Let's start with the very beginning of life. Look back and reflect on your childhood, beginning with your toddler years when you used to crawl around on the floor and continuing through kindergarten, elementary school, and middle school. When we think about what babies do, their main task is to search out their mothers' love. This appears to be instinctive. The hearts of babies are pure and unblemished, yet they are aware of love from the very beginning, and of their desire for it.

When babies feel unloved (when their mother goes away, or when they don't get what they want) they begin to cry, but when they feel loved (when they are caressed, or given milk or toys), they are extremely joyful. When we see this, we realize that not only do babies instinctively seek love, but they can also clearly tell whether they are being loved or not.

Between the ages of three and six, children begin to compare the amount of love they receive from their parents with the amount their brothers and sisters receive. Children of four or five years old might misbehave if they feel that their parents are giving all their love to a newborn brother or sister. Jealousy is an emotion that begins at a very early age. When we look at jealousy more closely, we see that it stems from a powerful desire to be loved. When this desire is not fulfilled, children react by causing mischief, and even real trouble. Love, then, seems to be a form of food, or nourishment, that is vital for us, starting in infancy.

As children move on from elementary school to middle school and then on to high school, they begin to look for love from friends and teachers as well. When children are praised by their teachers, or win the admiration of their friends for doing well in their studies, this gives them a feeling of satisfaction. Other children might become popular and feel loved because they excel in sports. Even teens who join gangs do so in search of acceptance and admiration, which are forms of love. Until we reach adulthood, we rely on winning the love and attention of others to provide us with a form of spiritual nourishment.

What happens when we reach adulthood? From our mid- to late twenties, both men and women think about marriage. To attract a mate, we study hard in college and strive to excel at academics or in our careers. Women exercise and wear beautiful clothes and makeup, searching for ways to make themselves appear more attractive. Men go to the gym and work hard at being successful. In all these activities, we see a more adult version of our need to win love.

From the instant we are born, we all have a strong desire for love, a natural craving that contains within it an element of selfishness. If we let that desire rule our lives from beginning to end, then everything we do will be driven by this hunger for love. Is this truly how we should lead our lives? This question leads us to the next aspect of love.

3. The Dynamics of Love

Now let's take a moment to look more deeply into the dynamics of love—the principles at work behind the actions and reactions associated with love. As we've seen, all babies thirst for love, and their parents are there to provide it to them. Parents do their best to offer their children love and affection. As time passes, these children grow into adulthood and have children of their own, and just as their parents did before them, they provide their children with love. (I don't mean to exclude grandparents from this picture, for it's very obvious that just having grandchildren is, in itself, a source of love and joy.)

As we look more closely, we see that love cannot be something that is always received from someone else. Somewhere, somehow, love must also be given. In families, receiving and giving love seems to move in cycles of twenty to thirty years. Parents give all their love to their children, and then these children grow up and have children of their own to whom they give their love and affection, and then the cycle repeats itself.

Thus far, we have been looking at love within the family,

but there is an equally important form of love that also drives us all: the love between men and women. From the age of around ten, we begin to develop an interest in the opposite sex, which, in our mid- to late teens, turns into a fascination that never seems to leave us. It is as if a powerful force is pulling men and women together like magnets, to the point where it becomes very difficult to think of anything else!

Soon enough, a sense of obligation, almost like an unspoken contract, emerges between men and women, although this sense of obligation is rarely something that we have been taught. Our instincts tell us that when we have a boyfriend or girlfriend, we shouldn't become too friendly with other boys, or other girls. Although no formal agreements have been made, a kind of pact emerges, part of the innate knowledge that love is a powerful bond. The love that men and women begin to experience from their teens into their twenties becomes the foundation on which they will build a marriage.

Matrimonial love is part of an exclusive relationship protected by law, into which nobody can intrude, at least not without consequences. When we observe a marital relationship, it looks as though exclusivity is part of the very nature of this love. For example, a husband or wife will feel very sad and lonely if his or her spouse goes out every night and returns home late. As you can see, there is a monopolistic element of love that leads to unhappiness when others intrude on that relationship.

4. A Prelude to Eternal Love

Now let's consider whether this possessive aspect of love is wrong. Some people believe that it is human nature to love all people equally, and that everyone should therefore be treated impartially. But what would happen if a woman was friendly to everyone regardless of who they were, and treated all the men she knew, including her husband, equally? And what would be the result if her husband were to treat all women in exactly the same way that he treats his wife? It is obvious that this couple would no longer be able to live together, and that their marriage would be destroyed.

One of the basic principles of marriage is that a married couple lives together, to ensure the stability that makes it possible to build a family and raise children. Long ago, Plato argued that the nation should take responsibility for raising and educating its children. However, this would reduce the purpose of our lives to biological reproduction; our only job would be the continuation of our species! This is not God's Will. God wants married couples to reap the rich harvest of spending many decades together, building a family, and supporting each other as they raise their children. The exclusive quality of matrimonial love may appear to arise from selfish desires for preservation and self-gratification, but these are minimal failings that we freely overlook in return for the love and the happiness we find in our families.

What appears to be self-serving is, in fact, part of the dynamic of creating something that exists in a higher dimension. The monopolistic aspect of the love between marriage partners can only be deemed destructive when it is taken to extremes—for example, when a partner's jealousy becomes so strong that it displaces respect for the dignity and freedom of the other person. A healthy dose of possessiveness between husband and wife is acceptable as long as it stays within reason and helps to hold the relationship together. But we should be careful not to let jealousy lead us to try to control our partner or to allow the relationship to become dominated by suspicion, because this is certain to lead to unhappiness.

Through our inquiry into romantic love, we have learned something about God's intentions. He encourages us—men and women—to find a partner, marry, and raise children, all in order to teach us about love. We have also seen that this love that springs between men and women, or between parents and children, is not necessarily everlasting or eternal. There is an instinctive aspect to this love, and, although the word "accidental" may not be quite appropriate in this context, there is no denying that some relationships do begin with a chance encounter that results in a blossoming of romance.

Is it part of God's design that this is all there is to love? No, of course not. He created romantic love as a way for all of us to awaken to a deeper form of love, and this has proved to be a very successful strategy. No matter how egotistical some people may be, they are still sure to feel attracted to the opposite sex and to experience love for their children. And what we feel toward the opposite sex and our own families gives us an opportunity to discover a higher form of love: eternal love. God has blessed us with basic human forms of love to help us awaken to the love that we will find in the higher dimensions of the spirit world.

5. For Whose Sake Do We Love?

The question I would like to pose now is this: "For whose sake do we love?" I mentioned that we know instinctively from earliest childhood that it is good to be loved and bad to be unloved. But if everybody is on the receiving end of love, there will be no one left to provide it. If there is only demand for love and no supply, then the world's reservoir of love will dry up, leaving a huge number of people thirsty.

When I look at this world on Earth through a spiritual lens, I see that we are all like travelers walking through a great desert. Many people are crying out for water as they stagger along under the burning sun. If they could only love each other, they would find that their thirst is eased. But they continue to think only of taking love from the people around them, and this makes their thirst grow stronger. When I look at the underlying spiritual state of the world and see this desert, it becomes easy to answer the question, "For whose sake do we love?" It is for our own sake that we should love others unconditionally. The paradoxical Truth is that giving love is the only way to get love. I am sure that you have heard the expression, "One good turn deserves another." When you do something helpful for someone else, the good that you do will go around and return to you some day. Love is very much the same; when you love others, you yourself will be loved.

Love is not found only between men and women, or within our families and among our relatives. In society, we find a kind of love between people who are not related by blood. The word "love" is quite strong and could be misleading in this context, but at the very least there are instances when others like or dislike us. People who are liked are indeed loved. If you think well of someone, look after that person, and are kind to that person, you are indeed giving that person your love.

Have you ever paused to consider the economics of love? In many ways, love resembles any other series of transactions. Let's look at a farmer. He grows vegetables and rice, which he takes to market and sells in exchange for money. Now he can use this money to buy the things he needs. If the farmer uses that money to buy a car, for instance, the automobile manufacturer will acquire money that he can then use to buy vegetables and rice. In this way, everything goes around in a circle. In economics, the value of one's work or labor is continuously circulating throughout society in the form of a medium we call money, or currency. It is the same with love. The love you give passes through several others before eventually returning to you. And the bottom line is this: you will receive as much as you have given.

In the same way that farmers are paid for the value of the rice they grow, or people in business are paid according to the amount of work they have done, those of us who have offered our love to others will receive a measure equal to what we have given. Although we may never receive it in a form that is tangible or visible in this three-dimensional world, there can be no disputing this Truth: love returns to those people who have given love to others.

The more we offer and give love, the more love we earn. This is why the spirits of the higher dimensions, the Great Guiding Spirits of Light who love a huge number of people, receive a tremendous amount of love themselves. So where does the love they receive come from? Is it found in the praises or blessings they receive from the people they love? It is to some extent, but that is not the whole story. The reward, the compensation for the love they have given, also comes back to them from God. It is bestowed on them through God's blessings.

6. The Essence of Salvation

I have mentioned that the seventh dimension is the world of love. We have also considered the various forms that love takes, including parental love, family love, and romantic love. So what kind of love is found among the spirits of the seventh dimension? Unlike the types of love that I have discussed so far, the love of the seventh dimension is not based on instinct. When the spirits of the seventh dimension are incarnated on Earth, their central task is to love others, whether or not they know them. As they dedicate themselves to enlightening people, they try to live as though God's Will were their own. This is their job on Earth, and also in the other world.

Many religions place a great deal of importance on the theme of salvation, on helping practitioners save others and become saved themselves. What then, is the essence of salvation? I mentioned earlier that when I consider this world on Earth through spiritual eyes, I see a scorching desert complete with plentiful mirages and desperate people staggering through the unbearable heat in search of water. In such a world, what will bring salvation? The answer must be something that will quench people's spiritual thirst. So what is it that people truly crave?

Two thousand years ago, Jesus Christ went to the daughter of a shepherd to ask for water to slake his thirst. As he drank the water, he said, "Everyone who drinks of this water will be thirsty again, but those who drink of the water that I will give them will never be thirsty. The water that I will give will become in them a spring of water gushing up to eternal life" (John 4:13-14). In these words, we can find the essence of salvation. What Jesus calls "the water that I will give" is the teachings that lead human souls to awaken to eternal life. This water is God's Truths. People who live according to God's Truths will never lose their way, never tire, and never thirst.

Countless travelers have been blessed by God's Truths. God's Truths have shown them how to live, and have given them the strength to persevere in the face of adversity. The power of God's Truths can be seen in their ability to awaken people and lead them to enlightenment and salvation. God's Truths are the essence of true love and true salvation. The work of bodhisattvas is to spread God's Truths far and wide, to protect people from thirst and offer them salvation.

7. The Lives of Giants in History

When we look over the history of humankind, we come across many great people who spent their lives serving as living forms of love, devoted to guiding others along the same path. These people's lives are worthy of our contemplation, for they provide shining examples for us to follow. The love they offered was not love as we know it, not the love that grows between man and woman, or between parent and child. In fact, their teachings express a love that stands in contrast to these more typical expressions.

Jesus Christ was one such person. When you think of his life from the perspective of filial love, he was far from being someone we would call a good child. Born the son of a carpenter, he was expected to follow his father's trade and become a skilled craftsman, marry, and raise children to carry on the family line. If he had followed this course, he would have been considered a very good son. But this was not the life he chose. And in addition to disobeying his father, he spoke sternly to his mother. He told her that our souls come from Heaven, not from other people; he asked her to understand, therefore, that though she was his physical mother, she did not give birth to his soul. From a worldly point of view, this was a very unkind thing to say.

Jesus did not get on very well with his four brothers, either. Unlike Jesus, they were very ordinary; of all the members of his family, Jesus was the only one who stood out. Neither his father, Joseph, nor his brothers could understand Jesus. They could not see why he went around saying all kinds of strange things and inspiring followers instead of helping build the family business. In truth, Jesus Christ was devoting his life to love on a higher plane; he was bringing salvation to the whole of humankind. Through the example of his life, we are re-minded that there are forms of love that transcend domestic love, brotherly love, and filial love.

The same can be said of the life of Gautama Siddhartha, the man who came to be venerated as the Buddha. He was born the son of a king, but he fled the Kapilavastu palace at the age of twenty-nine, leaving behind a wife and child, and turning a deaf ear to his father's entreaties. He became an ascetic; he spent six years in the mountains disciplining himself as he strove towards enlightenment.

Having been born a prince, Gautama Siddhartha had an obligation to succeed his father, the king, and lead the country, but he cast this duty aside. From a worldly point of view, he can only be described as a bad son. Furthermore, he had a wife named Yashodhara and a son named Rahula, whom he deserted. By not returning to Kapilavastu until he attained Great Enlightenment, Shakyamuni Buddha destroyed his marriage and ignored his obligations as a father. He did not set out to deny the value of parental and matrimonial love, but he was forced to break these bonds for the sake of a much higher ideal.

It would not have been possible for Gautama Siddhartha to attain enlightenment as the Buddha, or to preach the God's Laws to the people, so long as he lived in the royal palace as a prince. It should not be overlooked, however, that after his spiritual order was firmly established, he summoned his wife and child, accepted them as his disciples, and looked after them. He also welcomed many other men and women of his Shakya clan to his order. Despite earthly evidence to the contrary, he was a man with a strong sense of responsibility.

This would be an even more difficult world to live in if everyone was expected to seek a way of life that required them to cast aside their love for their spouses and children. Fortunately, this is not the case. If at all possible, we should pursue a form of universal love that can save the world while we continue to preserve the harmony of the home, the love between parents and children, and our jobs. However, we should never forget that among the great leaders in human history there have been exceptions to this ideal, people who embodied a form of love that went beyond earthly ties. These towering figures represent "love incarnate," and their lives continue to shine as brilliantly as the sun and stars, lighting our path. We should never stop paying homage to these giants for the sacrifices they made in pursuit of the noblest virtues.

8. Becoming Envoys of God's Love

What gave these two giants of human history the power to ignore worldly love and to seek something beyond it? Somehow, they understood the need to sacrifice the lesser values of this world for those of a higher plane. They knew that their love for God was far more valuable than their love for people. There is a vast difference between a life based on following the wavering, ever-changing minds of those around us, and a life based on love for the unchanging and everlasting Will of God. We express that eternal love through our efforts to become representatives of the mind of God. True love is found and expressed by living with God's mind, or His Will, as our own.

We cannot deny the importance of the love that exists between men and women, or of parental love, or of brotherly and sisterly love, and we should treasure these kinds of love for the blessings that they are. But we should also remember that these are instinctive forms of love, designed to prepare us to step up to a higher form of love: our love for God.

Let's take a closer look at two things, God's love for us, and our love of God. God loves every living thing; God embraces us with a vast, infinite love that knows no bounds. This is not a love that is given only when it is requested. It is not a love of give and take. It is an unconditional love, a love that never stops giving. Just as the sun supplies the Earth and all the plants and creatures living on it with a limitless amount of energy without seeking anything in return, God provides His pure, unremitting love, shining freely and gloriously as the greatest form of love we can ever know.

We should all be aware of God's love, and of how generously He gives it to us. If we forget to give thanks for this endless bounty, we can hardly call ourselves children of God. Surely it would be shameful to receive such a wonderful gift every single moment of every single day and still remain blind to it, but far too few people in this world express gratitude for the unconditional love of God. Most people are not even aware of the love they receive from Him.

We who are aware of His love, we who realize that God loves us, must find others with whom to share our knowledge of this love. When we become parents, we offer our children the same love our parents gave us. God is both Father and Mother of humankind, so surely we must find some place to share the love that we receive from Him. We should not give our love because we want to win praise or earn a good reputation; we should offer our love only because God loves us endlessly, and we should pass on that gift in the same spirit in which it is offered to us.

By looking through spiritual eyes, you can see that people are endlessly catching the waves of God's love the way a television antenna picks up signals from broadcasting stations. As long as we continue receiving God's love, we should aim to circulate it to the rest of the world. It is our duty to let the love flow through us and on to others; let the river's waters from on high flow downstream, all the way to the endless sea.

9. *Expanding Our Reservoirs of Love*

One way to imagine the soul is that it is like a pot that was designed to receive the love of God. If the pot is small, it will soon overflow, but a large pot will be able to retain an abundance of God's love. When the water in a dammed-up lake is released, it can turn massive turbines to generate electricity. It is the same with our souls; they house a reservoir that generates power according to the amount of love it holds.

The amount of love our souls can give depends on how big our reservoirs of love are. But size is not the only factor. Taller dams generate more power because their water falls for a longer distance. This is true of our souls, as well. Souls that possess an elevated awareness are capable of producing a larger amount of love. The largest reservoirs belong to the saviors of the ninth dimension. Incomparably vast, their store of love overflows with such force that it produces enough energy to supply the whole world.

If we wish to pursue the goal of becoming souls with a greater capacity to store love, we should strive to improve ourselves in two ways: by enlarging the vessel of the soul, and by raising our character to higher levels. To enlarge the vessel of our soul, we should make efforts to be as open-minded and forgiving as possible, and to cultivate a character that is so magnanimous that it can envelop and embrace everything.

To raise the level of our souls, we should work diligently to grow closer to God, step by step; this is the pursuit of enlightenment.

So what is enlightenment, exactly? What can we do to achieve enlightenment? Enlightenment is the sustenance for our souls that is acquired through our efforts to learn and practice God's Truths. This nourishment, and the experience it brings, is known as enlightenment. To successfully pursue enlightenment, we must try to absorb and practice the Truths as often as we can, manifesting them in our daily actions and spreading our love through them. This is how we will be able to cultivate greater magnanimity and raise the character of our souls, building within us a reservoir that is both large and tall.

10. Compassion – The Highest Form of Love

As we inquired into the love of the seventh dimension throughout this chapter, we found that love has more than one aspect. One kind of love exists between two or more people, between people and animals, and between people and plants; it exists within the relationship between any number of beings. This kind of love cannot exist in and of itself, completely on its own. A jewel gives off its shine whether or not someone is there to see it, but this relational form of love cannot exist that way. It is something that must be shared between one person or being and another, being given and then returned.

This relational love is not the only form of love, however. There is also a kind of love that sparkles in the morning sun all on its own. This kind of love far surpasses the love between people, animals, and plants, or the love we have for objects. What, then, is this quality that is greater than ordinary love? We have called it God's love, but another word for it is "compassion." Compassion surpasses love. A diamond glimmers brilliantly, but not because it expects something in return; it simply gives off its shine eternally. This is also true of the highest form of love, known as compassion, the unconditional love that never stops giving.

Sometimes, when we walk through mountain valleys, we may come across beautiful azaleas or violets blossoming in colorful splendor from cracks in the rocks. Why do the flowers look so beautiful? Why do flowers bloom at all? Lilies bloom in the valleys for the sake of blooming, just as diamonds shine for the sake of shining, but they also give us a chance to think about the importance of simple existence. I see within them something that does not give and receive, but only gives and gives. Their very existence is compassionate. Compassion has value in and of itself, whether or not anyone or anything else is there to experience it, and in this way, compassion transcends ordinary love.

Compassion is found when a person gives love just by existing, when he or she only has to be present to provide love. This form of love represents a state close to God. God, through His very existence, provides love to all creatures. Compassion surpasses love between human beings and represents the highest goal we can strive to attain.

WHAT ARE THEY DOING NOW IN HEAVEN?

~EINSTEIN, CARNEGIE,

MOZART, AND PICASSO~

•

Not all Divine Spirits involve themselves in religious work. Many of them are engaged in a variety of professions as they discipline themselves in this earthly world. No matter what profession we work in, if we work for the sake of the people of the world, we will be working in accordance with God's Will and practicing His Truths.

There are numerous scientists, businessmen, and artists, as well as people in all other genres of work, who belong to the higher dimensions of the spirit world. For instance, Albert Einstein lives in the eighth dimension where he still continues with his studies in physics. Among the businessmen now living in the World of Bodhisattvas, we find the car manufacturer Henry Ford, the steel magnate Andrew Carnegie, and the financial tycoon John D. Rockefeller. They are now working on the theme of modern society and management. Among the artists, Picasso is now active in the Brahma Realm, the highest part of the seventh dimension. In the field of music, Johann Sebastian Bach lives in the World of Tathagatas of the eighth dimension, where he is composing heavenly music. Mozart lives in the World of Bodhisattvas, where he is working on Christian music. Beethoven lives in the lower area of the World of Bodhisattvas. He now aims to transcend the sadness evident in parts of his music and become an expert in the music of joy.

5

THE WORLD
OF THE
EIGHTH DIMENSION

1. Who Are the Tathagatas?

Like the word *bodhisattva*, *tathagata* is a Buddhist term; in Japanese, it means "coming from the Eternal Truths" or "embodying the absolute Truths of God." It is difficult to generalize about tathagatas' level of spiritual awareness, but we know that they come from the world of transcendental wisdom, and that when they incarnate on Earth, they achieve great prominence in human history. Tathagatas are the equivalent of archangels in Christianity. These inhabitants of the eighth dimension are sometimes referred to as Great Guiding Spirits of Light.

The total population of the spirit world is about fifty billion, but fewer than five hundred of these spirits are tathagatas. This works out to an average of approximately one tathagata per one hundred million people. The population of Japan is presently one hundred twenty million, so if the ratio is the same in this world as in the spirit world, then there may be only one tathagata in the entire country of Japan, if that.

At some periods of history, however, higher Truths are taught on a grand scale; at these times, more tathagatas are born. This makes it difficult to determine exactly how many tathagatas are on Earth at any given time. In any age, however, there are never more than several tathagatas living on Earth at the same time, and perhaps this is how it should be. Tathagatas stand out from their contemporaries like Mount Fuji, the highest mountain in Japan, stands out from the rest of the country. Standing alone, Mount Fuji is very impressive, and inspires awe in the beholder because of the way it towers above its surroundings. Similarly, the stature of tathagatas is such that they soar above all others, contributing to the beauty of an otherwise flat landscape.

When a major civilization is reaching its peak, tathagatas are born on Earth in succession, one after another. For instance, in ancient Greek civilization, Socrates was a tathagata, as was his disciple, Plato. Plato's student, Aristotle, was also a tathagata. Another tathagata who lived in Greece at about the same time was Pythagoras, who was followed by Archimedes (a Grand Spirit of the ninth dimension; Grand Spirits are always tathagatas, but the converse is not always true). The early Chinese civilization saw the appearance of Confucius (a Grand Spirit of the ninth dimension), Lao-tzu, Chuang-tzu, and Mo-tzu, who were all tathagatas. Jesus Christ (a Grand Spirit of the ninth dimension), and John the Baptist were both tathagatas, and among the prophets of the Old Testament, Jeremiah and Elijah were tathagatas. Of course, Shakyamuni Buddha, a Grand Spirit of the ninth dimension who founded the Buddhist religion, was also a tathagata, as were several of his followers.

Tathagatas appear on Earth to elevate a particular culture to its pinnacle. They help a civilization reach new heights by teaching the fundamental Truths or becoming active leaders in cultural or artistic fields. Eventually, when the culture they helped create falls into decline, various bodhisattvas come down to breathe new life into it. When the civilization finally faces its end, tathagatas appear again to create a new culture. This cycle has been repeated over and over throughout the course of history.

2. The Nature of Light

When you enter the eighth dimension, you will be struck by the abundance of light. *Light* is a word that people use in a variety of ways, often without being aware of its meaning. At Happy Science, we say, "God is light, and so as children of God, human beings are also essentially light" or "The Divine Spirits carry out their missions so they can manifest the seven-colored light of God." But what exactly *is* this light? What do we mean when we say "God is light?"

Certainly if we were to list the qualities of light, we could begin by saying that it is bright and that it is the source of life energy. Light is a positive entity, an active expression of energy; it has its own will and purpose. Another way of defining light is to contrast it with its opposite state. This, of course, is darkness. Darkness is characterized by the absence of light, visibility, brightness, hope, and vitality. When we talk about light and darkness in this way, we once again come up against the question of dualism.

Is darkness merely the absence of light, or does darkness exist in and of itself? Darkness does not have its own independent existence. Darkness is created only when something blocks rays of light. For example, night exists only when the Earth's rotation blocks the sunlight. No matter how strong a light may be, if something blocks it, darkness will result. The nature of light is to go straight ahead, so if something obstructs its way, it gets blocked. And the stronger the light, the deeper the darkness. Even if we were to shine a million candlepower spotlight on a rock, that light would not illuminate the space behind it; in fact, the darkness this brilliant spotlight would create would actually be deeper than that created by a lesser light.

The same can be said of good and evil. They both exist, but good exists as an active, independent entity, whereas evil has a passive, dependent existence. Although evil does not have an independent existence, it shows up whenever lack of goodness creates the appropriate conditions. Evil comes into being through the intervention of a third party—like the rock that blocked the light. And just as darkness provides a contrast to light, evil appears wherever there is good, and makes the good stand out.

Even if you were to illuminate a room in your home with an extremely bright lamp, you would not be able to avoid shadows forming somewhere in the room. Of course, if the room were walled with mirrors, there would be no shadows, but in ordinary circumstances, shadows are sure to form, no matter how well a place may be lit; furniture and other household objects will block the light and create shadows. Shadows, darkness, and evil do not exist in themselves; they come into being in the natural course of everyday life.

3. The Nature of Space

As a way of exploring the nature of light at greater depth, let's look at the issue of space. What is space? This is a question that people throughout the ages have posed. Space may be described as having height, width, and depth that make it three-dimensional, like a box. This is one definition, but it is not entirely correct. This definition does not include the spirit world—which consists of the fourth, fifth, sixth, seventh, and eighth dimensions and beyond.

The true nature of space extends far beyond the three dimensions that dominate our everyday life on Earth. Space is essentially a field of energy, or consciousness, that can take all kinds of actions. As a result of these actions, all phenomena emerge—those that we can perceive as well as those that we cannot. Space provides a dwelling place for the light of God. Space is the field of consciousness where God's light can create infinitely complex phenomena and take a multitude of actions in many different dimensions.

4. In the Flow of Eternal Time

Time is a concept that is often compared to space; it is often said that space represents a horizontal expansion whereas time is a vertical expansion. But what is the relationship between time and space? Can space exist without time?

That light is active implies movement of some kind, and movement in turn requires the passage of time. Would it be possible for light to remain active if time were to stop? The answer is no; if time were to come to a halt, light would also become inert. In order for space to carry out its role as an

energy field, time must be inherent within it. We can therefore come to the following conclusions: space cannot exist
without time; time and space cannot be separated; and it is
the ongoing existence of space that allows light to play its role
in the universe.

There is more to light than meets the eye. Light can be
broken down into *photons*, which are the building blocks of all
Creation. These photons can take the form of waves or particles. Everything in the universe is made up of these particles, which means that all material objects, including human
beings, are essentially made of light. When light takes on
particle form, it creates material objects, and when it does
not, it forms the spiritual energy that exists in the fourth
dimension and those above it; this energy is the basis of spiritual existence. This means everything in the universe—on
Earth and in the dimensions beyond—is made of light.

Space comes into existence only when light becomes
active. Space cannot exist without the activities of light.
Without time, light is unable to be active, which means that
without time there would be no space, no material objects,
no spirits, nothing. This makes time an essential component
of existence. The world that God created, that is to say, the
third, fourth, fifth, sixth, seventh, and eighth dimensions and
beyond, consists of space that encompasses time as well as
the light that moves within this space. When God created
the world, He did so using these three elements: light, space,

and time. Light transforms itself to create matter and the spiritual bodies that inhabit all the dimensions. Light needs space in which to be active. And light needs time to travel through space.

5. Achieving Evolution and Harmony

When we understand the true nature of the world that surrounds us, we begin to know why we are alive, how we should live, and what we should aim for in our lives. Only by clearly seeing the world God created can we discover principles that will guide us through our lives. What are these principles? We can discover them by understanding God's plan for the world and for our lives.

So what kind of world did God intend to create with the three elements of light, space, and time? If we imagine that space is like a transparent glass box and that a beam of light shines in from one corner, we can see that this light will reflect off the inner surfaces of the box and bounce around the interior forever. Through its endless movement, light constantly creates different shapes and images. When we look at the history of the universe and humanity from this perspective, we realize that this light was not introduced merely as the product of chance, but that its arrival was part of a purposeful plan. The light that the Primordial God emitted is not just moving around randomly: it has the clear objective of serving the progress of humankind and the universe.

God's light has two primary objectives. The first of these is evolution. When we look at the history of Earth, the history of humankind, and the history of the universe itself, we discover the great force of evolution at work in them all. Only because we strive to attain a higher level of development are we given life. This is why we have been given the blessing of life. If humankind only degenerated over time, we would have to question the very meaning of our existence. Why should we exist at all if we are only becoming more and more corrupt?

For example, we could find great joy in working with clay because it is a process of creating something out of nothing, but it would lose all meaning if the animals and humans you created out of clay only ended up as lumps of clay in the end. The true nature of evolution is to make something out of nothing, to transform the intangible into the tangible. To make something out of nothing and then to develop it into something even greater is one of the objectives of humankind.

The second objective is to create harmony, a great and grand harmony. What do I mean by grand harmony? Imagine that God created a mountain of clay in a vast room, then out of this clay He created the sun, the Earth, the moon, plants, animals, human beings and all kinds of other things.

It is wonderful that the intangible evolved into the tangible in this way, but now we have to establish whether these creations can co-exist in an orderly and beautiful way. God decided to create harmony between them—balance between plants, animals, and human beings, between day and night, between land and sea, between hot and cold, and between the sun, the Earth, the moon, and all the other planets and stars. When we look at the course of human history, we can see that humans have been striving to fulfill God's Will and to achieve His two primary objectives: evolution and harmony.

6. What Are the Laws?

If the primary guiding principles for humankind are evolution and harmony, then what are the Truths that people have been seeking through the ages? And how do the Laws work as a system that supports the Truths?

The Laws are rules that govern the universe; they are God's Truths manifested in the form of a system. The two elements of evolution and harmony are contained within the Laws. Personal improvement, or the development of the individual, is an integral element of the Laws. Any Law that does not work for the improvement of the individual is not a true Law; it is not part of the Truths of God. It never has been and never will be. The principle of progress, or the principle of evolution, is inherent in the Laws, so at the very least, the Laws must promote individual growth and raise spiritual awareness.

The improvement of individuals is the ultimate good, but when all of us have the freedom to do what we like to improve ourselves (free will), this can lead to conflict. This is why we need a Law that resolves such conflicts in a way that leads to the improvement of the community. Let's consider an example: a person wants to be president of the company he works for, but there are two other executives who also feel that same way. All three cannot hold the post at once, so the board of trustees must evaluate all three to see who has what it takes. If there is only one person suitable for this task, he will be given the post and the other two will not. If all three applicants are suitable for the job, the board will have to decide who should become the president first, and make arrangements so that the other two will have an opportunity to become president as well. In this way, the development of the individual is balanced against the good of the whole, arriving at harmony.

Numerous religious leaders, moralists, and philosophers throughout history have taught variations on this basic principle of harmony. China's most famous philosopher, Confucius, espoused the seniority system based on his belief that young people should respect their elders and defer to them. According to his philosophy, if the three people who wanted to become president were equal in their abilities, then the job should be awarded to the eldest. This system still exists, to some extent, to this day. Even though age does not necessarily correspond to spiritual development, people still tend to assume that if two people are equally talented, then the more experienced one should possess greater wisdom. This assumption lies at the heart of the seniority system.

We should also be aware of another variation, known as the merit system. In the merit system, the person with the greatest ability and the strongest skills is chosen for advancement. Other philosophers advocate utilitarianism, as put forward by Jeremy Bentham, which aims for "the greatest happiness for the greatest number." John Stuart Mill also supported this approach.

The need to develop the individual in order to benefit society as a whole is expressed in the Laws, which combine the two Buddhist philosophies of the Small Vehicle (Hinayana) and the Great Vehicle (Mahayana). The Small Vehicle, which focuses on the enlightenment of the individual, embodies the principle of progress, whereas the Great Vehicle incorporates the principle of harmonizing conflicting needs as the basis for building a Utopia in this world. Thus the Laws contain two main principles, evolution and harmony, and it is through the balance of these principles that humanity as a whole can achieve happiness.

7. God's Compassion for Humankind

I teach that the pursuit of happiness is part of human nature, and that this happiness we seek has two aspects—personal happiness and public happiness. Personal happiness probably needs no explanation, but by public happiness I mean that once you have achieved personal happiness, you can share your happiness with others and spread it to society, the world, and humankind as a whole. I believe working to this end— working towards Utopia in this world—should be our goal. This is the fundamental objective of our spiritual movement. God in His mercy has bestowed a purpose on humankind. If this purpose were to promote unhappiness, the world would be a wretched place indeed. However, God implanted within our souls the desire to strive for happiness, making this an integral part of what makes us human.

You may wonder why we seek happiness in the first place. It is because God Himself pursues happiness, and we, who are children of God, possess the same essential nature. We are children of God's light, aspects of the great force that embodies the energy of happiness and governs the universe. Just as the pursuit of happiness is the very purpose of God's existence, it is also the reason for ours.

So what is it that gives God happiness? What makes Him feel joy? The perfect balance between evolution and harmony.

God finds happiness in the process of producing, nurturing, developing, and bestowing prosperity on all of Creation while establishing a grand harmony among them. As long as God is active in this process, as long as He manifests His aim to bring harmony to all Creation, allowing it to progress and prosper, God will experience joy and pleasure.

In this way, God Himself undergoes transformation, always becoming greater, always continuing to expand and develop Himself. Human beings were created to live in happiness by making their own contribution to evolution and harmony; this reality indicates the true nature of God, and is in itself evidence of His great compassion.

8. The Roles of Tathagatas

In *The Laws of the Sun*, I stated that the Primordial God created all souls equal, but that He also looks at souls from a perspective of fairness, evaluating them according to their capabilities and achievements. Part of this fairness means that those who have developed the qualities of leadership are given suitable positions, roles, and power. The superior rank of the tathagata is based on this principle of fairness.

Although we are born equal as children of God, those who have succeeded in accumulating wisdom through repeated incarnations on Earth are given a special position so that they can achieve even greater self-realization. The Primordial God does not take a human form: He is the force that created this vast, multi-dimensional universe, and it is beyond our ability to see Him as a physical being. Tathagatas, therefore, act in His stead, so that we can feel the greatness of God. In other words, tathagatas exist to let human beings experience the existence of God in the way they can. This is why tathagatas are said to embody "love incarnate." Tathagatas function as God's representatives.

Tathagatas are the embodiment of the absolute Truths, which means that their very existence expresses their love for humans. In other words, tathagatas exist to guide us to the path of enlightenment, help us attain higher awareness, and lead us to happiness. Tathagatas are the personification of God's light. It is impossible for humans to see, understand, or comprehend God Himself, but we can infer the existence of God through the tathagatas, His representatives. They exist to provide us with a living metaphor for God, and to allow us to experience His compassion and His power. In this way, tathagatas serve as great teachers who guide humankind to the path of happiness.

LOVE INCARNATE

•

The love that tathagatas give is love incarnate. It expresses the light of God; it is no longer a one-to-one love, but a love for everyone. A person who has become a tathagata radiates boundless love in all directions, and that person's existence itself is love. This is the love embodied by the great figures whose names have lasted throughout history, such as the great Greek philosopher Socrates, who has influenced 2,400 years of history. In recent years, other great figures have brought light to the world, including the great humanitarian Albert Schweitzer (1875–1965) and Thomas Edison (1847–1931), who contributed to the advancement of science and technology. The very existence of these great figures is an expression of love for all humanity.

The goal of your spiritual training on Earth is to progress through the different stages of love to become love incarnate, so that your very existence is a blessing to all humankind. When you live with this love, you are living not merely as a human being, but as a representative of God, a manifestation of light. This is the kind of love that will open a new era for humanity.

9. Conveying God's Light

Ultimately, the role of the tathagata is to convey who God is. As God's representatives, tathagatas have the authority to speak on behalf of God. Because tathagatas are much closer to God than ordinary people are, they are also allowed to teach others about God. As Great Guiding Spirits of Light that reside in the eighth dimension, tathagatas have permission to describe His existence in great detail. However, even tathagatas are unable to teach everything about God. The soul of a single human being, no matter how advanced, is incapable of grasping the full greatness of God. This is why the tathagatas of the eighth dimension are divided into separate groups, each one representing the qualities of a single color, or aspect, of the light of God.

I will explain the different colors of God's light in greater detail in the next chapter, but at this point, it's helpful to know that tathagatas who belong to the group of the golden light, led by Gautama Siddhartha, describe God through the aspects of enlightenment, the Laws, and compassion, whereas tathagatas who belong to the group of the white light, guided by Jesus Christ, teach about God from the standpoint of love. Those of the red light, governed by Moses, try to teach who God is through the miracles that He performs. Tathagatas of the green light, as represented by the Chinese philosophers Lao-tzu and Chuang-tzu, teach how we can see the existence of God in nature, and in the harmony that exists there. Tathagatas that belong to the blue light of Zeus reveal God through artwork. Tathagatas of the violet light are guided by Confucius and let us feel God through the teachings of propriety, order, and loyalty and by inspiring reverence towards God. Through these teachings, tathagatas let us experience various aspects of God.

As we have seen, each group of tathagatas basically teaches us the same thing—the nature of God—but they do so through the perspective of the particular color of light to which they belong. Throughout history, human beings have fought wars over differences in religion because they were not aware that these different Guiding Spirits of Light all teach aspects of the same Truth. They did not understand the roles these different tathagatas play. As a result, they denounced the followers of religions different from their own as heretics, and fought against them. Now, however, the time has come for humankind to gain a true understanding of God by recognizing that the works and the teachings of various tathagatas represent different colors of one divine light.

10. The Path to Perfection

I have described tathagatas as beings much greater than the rest of humankind. But does this mean that they have completed their spiritual training? Is there nothing left for them to learn? The truth is that they still need to undergo spiritual training on Earth as human beings. While they reside in the eighth dimension, tathagatas are the embodiment of their unique color of spiritual light. But through the process of coming down to Earth every few hundred or few thousand years in the cycle of reincarnation, they experience life as human beings and continue to learn a multitude of things. While they live in this three-dimensional world, they are exposed to viewpoints other than their own and learn teachings and thoughts that belong to different colors of spiritual light. The purpose of their spiritual training on Earth is to enhance their insight and deepen their understanding of the world. Tathagatas devote themselves to understanding humankind, the Truths, and history from an ever-higher, broader, and more integrated perspective. In this respect, even though they are tathagatas—and are therefore much closer to perfection than the rest of humankind—they are still walking on the path to enlightenment.

God created the system of reincarnation as a way for humans to evolve and develop themselves. No soul is exempt from this system. Although some will argue to the contrary, even the tathagatas are not exempt from this rule. They cannot reside in the spirit world indefinitely, and they will reincarnate at some point. But they have achieved an extraordinary degree of freedom: they are able to choose when and where they wish to be reincarnated in accordance with their own plans. This is what it means when we say that tathagatas have achieved liberation from the constraint of reincarnation.

By contrast, souls that reside in the seventh dimension and lower are sent down to live on Earth as necessary. They are obliged to be born in various eras as part of their spiritual education. While souls in the lower dimensions are more like students obligated to study in school, tathagatas are like graduates who have finished a set course of spiritual education and are free to choose what and when they would like to study. Their goal is to achieve a global, universal perspective. To achieve this perspective, the tathagatas walk the path to perfection through their own spiritual discipline.

6

THE WORLD
OF THE
NINTH DIMENSION

·

1. The World Beyond the Veil

In the previous chapters, I have revealed the structure of the spirit world from the fourth to the eighth dimensions, and I have explained the laws and systems of these worlds. Very few people in the history of humankind have described them as vividly and clearly as I have, and it is my earnest hope that what I have revealed will help many people understand the invisible world beyond. Now I will do my best to reveal the mysteries of the ninth dimension, piercing the veil that has shrouded this dimension and kept it hidden from human-kind behind a cloud of mysticism. The Truths of God that I will reveal here have been concealed from even the most renowned philosophers and leaders of religion. This world of the highest divinities of Earth is so mystical that it is almost beyond human comprehension, but I will try to explain it in the simplest way I can.

The world of the ninth dimension is the world of saviors, or Grand Tathagatas, and it is limited to ten inhabitants. These are the spirits we consider messiahs, who come down to this world no more than once every several thousand years. Depending on the era, these ninth-dimensional spirits may or may not decide to descend to Earth. Some of them may appear on Earth several times within a given era, while others may choose not to appear at all. The inhabitants of the ninth dimension discuss their roles together, and determine which combination of spirits will appear on Earth in a given time span. This is how each era, or civilization, acquires its unique characteristics.

Among the residents of the ninth dimension who are most famous today are Gautama Siddhartha, Jesus Christ, and Moses. Another well-known being of the ninth dimension, although he is not usually referred to as a savior, is Confucius. One thing all the spirits in the ninth dimension have in common is that during their incarnations on Earth, they established the very principles that gave rise to our great civilizations.

2. The World of Wonder

The ninth dimension is a very mysterious and mystical place, but one thing is certain: its inhabitants are no longer completely human. This will be easier to understand if I put it in context by reviewing the forms that souls of other dimensions take in their worlds. The fourth and fifth dimensions are very easy to grasp, because their inhabitants take on human-like form. Although the spirits in the fourth dimension are living in their astral bodies, their lifestyle strongly resembles the way they used to live on Earth in physical bodies. The same is true of those who dwell in the fifth dimension; many of these spirits continue working in the same occupations they had on Earth, for example, as carpenters, schoolteachers, merchants, mechanics, or farmers. In the sixth dimension, where god-like souls live, spirits possess a much higher level of awareness. Most of the time they continue to look human, like the souls of the lower dimensions. But once in a while, they will remember that their true nature is consciousness, which is capable of flying anywhere they desire. When this happens, wings might appear on souls with a Western background, and those with an Asian background might ride on top of little floating clouds. So the way the souls in the sixth dimension live is somewhat different from the way we live on Earth with our five senses.

The spirits in the seventh dimension possess an even higher awareness of their spiritual nature. For the most part, these spirits continue to adopt a human appearance, but the tasks they take on are without bounds, and in this sense, they no longer maintain lifestyles that resemble ones we have on Earth. Their lifestyles focus on paying frequent visits to the lower dimensions of the spirit world to teach and guide the spirits there; they do not stay in the seventh dimension but travel around freely to fulfill their duties. These spirits also work tirelessly to provide guidance from Heaven to make the third dimension a better place. The lifestyle in this dimension is clearly very different from life on Earth, but because spirits in this dimension have not yet reached the level of awareness of tathagatas, they still try to remember what they looked like on Earth in order to see themselves objectively.

The World of Tathagatas, the eighth dimension, is a bit different. Once in a while, tathagatas visit Earth as Guiding Spirits for religious leaders. When they do, they take on a godly appearance. For instance, when the Shinto god Ame-no-Minakanushi-no-Mikoto (the Lord God of the Heavenly Center) manifested himself as the Lord of Seicho-No-Ie, a modern Japanese sect, he did so in the form of an elderly, white-haired man.

In their daily lives in the other world, however, tathagatas do not normally assume a human appearance because it is no longer relevant to them. Sometimes they take on human appearance during conversations with other spirits of their own world to make it easier to identify each other, but this is not typical. In fact, they are capable of transforming their appearance into anything they want, including dividing themselves into more than one body to achieve a specific goal. They are capable of splitting into as many separate entities as necessary and of transforming into various images. There is a famous Chinese novel about the Monkey King, who could take one of his hairs and make it transform into an elephant or into a copy of himself. This might help you understand what the souls in the eighth dimension are capable of. They can split off parts of their consciousness, of their light, and this allows them to perform many tasks simultaneously to fulfill their unique responsibilities.

Thus far, I have described the various worlds up to the eighth dimension. The ninth, however, is a very mysterious world that can be difficult for the human imagination to accept, limited as we are by what we experience on Earth. I have said that ten people live in the ninth dimension, but rather than thinking of them as people, it might be more helpful to think of them as ten gigantic spheres of light, each with its own individual characteristics and personality. When they communicate with me on Earth, they adopt the appearance and character they possessed during an incarnation on Earth, but they usually do not take on human form.

It is difficult to describe how this occurs, but I will attempt to do so using the metaphor of electricity. The spirits of the ninth dimension are like ten batteries, each with its own particular characteristics. Each battery is attached to a wire that connects its positive and negative terminals, and this wire has many Christmas-tree lights connected to it. When electricity flows through these lightbulbs, they light up. Although there are many lightbulbs on this wire, they are all connected to the same battery and draw their energy from the same electrical source. For example, one of the batteries, the Great Buddha Consciousness, has a light bulb named La Mu, another light bulb named Rient Arl Croud, and still others known as Hermes and Gautama Siddhartha. When necessary, these sparkling light bulbs give off different colors to express themselves in different personalities.

3. *The Light of Ninth-Dimensional Spirits*

As we've discussed, the inhabitants of the ninth dimension don't usually take on human appearance. So, contrary to popular wisdom, they don't sit on thrones in a heavenly palace, wearing crowns and long white robes. These spirits of the ninth dimension are better described as electromagnetic forces, or energy bodies with consciousnesses, and it is in this form that they carry out their daily activities. When one of the spirits turns on one of its many light bulbs, people become capable of recognizing it based on its unique shape and color.

When Jesus inhabits the ninth-dimensional world, he does not take on the human form with which we are all familiar: the slender young man with long hair and a beard. He appears as a mass of light that expresses the characteristics of Jesus. When necessary, this sphere of light sends guidance to people on Earth or to the spirits of the eighth dimension and below.

Only when Jesus speaks to the tathagatas of the eighth dimension or the bodhisattvas of the seventh dimension does he take on the form he adopted when he lived on Earth, which makes him easier to recognize. The only spirits capable of seeing him in this guise are those who dwell in the eighth or seventh dimensions, as well as some who dwell in the sixth dimension. When the inhabitants of lower dimensions look at him, they will only see a dazzling, radiant light, too bright to gaze upon directly.

I have described each of the dimensions and their similarities and differences in many ways, but when it comes right down to it, the ultimate difference can be found in the amount of light that the spirits possess. This is not the ordinary light we are used to seeing, for it has unique qualities that appear as bundles of yellow, white, red, and green rays. This is what they really look like. Of course, when I speak of yellow, white, red, or green lights, I am only using words that can be understood here on Earth.

On Earth, color, in its true sense, does not exist. What we think of as blue is not really blue at all; it is merely a surface reflecting back the blue rays of the sun's light spectrum. Something that absorbs all the sun's rays appears black to us, while something that reflects them all appears white. Something that reflects only the yellow rays appears yellow. In this way, nothing on Earth really has any color of its own; all objects in this world are merely made of particles that reflect a certain color of light, making them *appear* colored.

It is easy to observe that color doesn't really exist here on Earth. All you have to do is turn off the lights and you will see that nothing is capable of retaining its color without light. If a color really existed, we should be able to see it even in the dark, but the truth is that all things that have a particular color are simply reflecting certain wavelengths of light, and they disappear when there is no light to reflect.

4. The Purpose of Religion

In my description of the eighth dimension, I said that in this dimension the light of God is split, as if it had passed through a prism, and that each ray of light represents different teachings and characteristics of God. Each of the tathagatas taught according to his or her own understanding of God, and these teachings developed into the religions we find all over the world. But why was it necessary to have different religions? I am sure that many people might think that it would have been better if there was only one way of representing God. This certainly would have helped avoid all the confusion, religious conflict, and chaos we see around the world today.

While this idea looks good on the surface, many mistaken ideas and dangers are actually hidden within it. If humankind were presented with a "ready-to-wear," "one-size-fits-all" religion, would we really be satisfied? When you look at a highway, you see a wide array of different cars of various shapes, sizes, and colors. Many different manufacturers and models are available, calculated to appeal to a wide range of budgets and other needs.

Why do we have such a wide variety of cars? It is because a car is much more than just a means of transporting people or things. A car plays another important role—it acts as a symbolic stand-in for its owner, as a way of representing its owner's interests and personality. It may indicate that the owner is a practical kind of person, or that the owner is interested in status, or that the owner is single, or married with a large family.

As you can see, even with something as simple as a car, it is impossible to say that any one model is the best. There are a plethora of religions in the world today, which causes a lot of confusion, but we can no more say which religion is the right one than we can say which car is best. Of course, we can generalize and say that the more expensive the car, the better the quality, but this does not necessarily mean that it will appeal to everyone's tastes and needs. Taste varies from person to person, and we can never say that any one specific car is the right one for all people; it is good to have differences.

As we saw in the last chapter, Buddhism has two schools of thought, the Hinayana, also known as the Small Vehicle, and Mahayana, also known as the Great Vehicle. The Small Vehicle can be thought of as a small car that can only carry you, the driver, whereas the Great Vehicle is like a bus that can carry a large number of passengers. In the same way that there are various vehicles in different sizes to suit many people's needs, religions also adapt themselves to people's tastes, local cultures, and regional qualities.

In biblical lands, where war and destruction were commonplace, people needed a god who would teach them about justice. In the Far East, a god who would teach about harmony was necessary. In Western civilizations, where cultures are based on rationalism, spiritual teachings took the form of philosophy. The objective of religion is to transport people from one place to another, from this world to those beyond it, in whatever form may be required. The vehicles that carry people between these places may be many and varied, but no matter which one we ride, we will discover joy and a sense of purpose. This is how the system has been designed by God.

5. The Seven Colors of God's Light

God's light is expressed through seven colors. In the ninth dimension, the light of God is divided into these seven colors through each of the Grand Tathagatas of this dimension. As the light flows downwards, these seven colors of light are transmitted to the many tathagatas residing in the eighth dimension, where the light is split still further to produce more than twenty different colors.

The first of the seven colors in the ninth dimension is yellow, which shines with a golden hue. It is governed by Gautama Siddhartha, otherwise known as Shakyamuni Buddha. Buddha's yellow light is the color of God's Laws, of compassion. White light is regulated by Jesus Christ. This is the color of love. Spirits who are involved in medicine or other forms of healing receive the guidance of this white light. Can it be mere coincidence that doctors and nurses wear white uniforms?

Moses is in charge of red light, the color that instructs people who are considered leaders in society. Political leaders and those who contribute to guiding society towards justice fall under the influence of this red light. Red light is also referred to as the light of miracles, because whenever miraculous or inexplicable phenomena occur, they do so under the auspices of this red light.

Next we come to blue light. This is the color of philosophy and ideology, and it is controlled not by one spirit, but by two. The first is Zeus, who, when he appeared in ancient Greece, was primarily in charge of the arts and literature. (The arts also fall under the influence of green light.) The other spirit in charge of blue light is Manu, who according to Indian mythology was the progenitor of the human race. His philosophy was the basis for the "Laws of Manu" (or Manu Smriti), which prescribes the daily conduct of the Brahman caste. Manu is responsible for philosophical matters, but also handles many special assignments, including various global racial issues, such as unifying the belief systems of different races and nations.

Silver light is the light of science and modernization. This color is under the regulation of the spirit who previously incarnated as Isaac Newton, and who sometime before that was born as Archimedes. Although he is a Grand Tathagata of the ninth dimension, he appeared on Earth as a scientist to promote scientific advancements in the third dimension and above. Thomas Edison and Albert Einstein are both tathagatas of the eighth dimension who work under the silver light.

Next, we come to the green light, which governs nature and harmony. This color is controlled jointly by the ninth-dimensional spirits Manu, who also governs blue light, and Zoroaster (Zarathustra), a god of the Middle East and founder of a Persian religion that believed in the duality of good and evil, and that used fire in its worship. Both of these spirits teach the workings of nature on Earth, as well as the structure and harmony of the whole universe. You may have heard of Lao-tzu and Chuang-tzu; green light guides the philosophies of these spirits of the eighth dimension.

Finally, violet light comes under the direction of Confucius. This light deals with ethics and morals, scholarly thinking, propriety, and order. It provides a way of organizing the world in hierarchical order, and of promoting a system of control based on seniority. The gods of the Japanese Shinto religion fall under the influence of this light.

I have now introduced you to eight Grand Tathagatas, and explained how each of them governs one of the seven colors of God's Light. However, we know that there are ten Grand Tathagatas who live in the ninth dimension. So who are the remaining two spirits, and what do they do? One of these spirits is Enlil, who was known in the Middle East by the name of Yahweh. He is the god of the Israelites, and he is also feared as the god of disaster in the Far East. The other Grand Tathagata is Maitrayer, whose role is coordinating and regulating. He is responsible for splitting God's light, as well as adjusting the strength of each of the colors to achieve balance.

6. The Role of Shakyamuni Buddha

Among these spirits of the ninth dimension, there is one leading, central spirit. This life force was once incarnated in India as Gautama Siddhartha, also known as Shakyamuni Buddha. When Shakyamuni Buddha appeared on Earth, however, his incarnating spirit housed only one-fifth of the power that he possesses in the ninth dimension, where he is known as the Great Buddha Consciousness. The Great Buddha Consciousness, or the core spirit of the Shakyamuni Consciousness, is called El Cantare Consciousness. In the ninth dimension, El Cantare Consciousness is a tremendously large spirit. This spirit has a very long history as the oldest and most venerable consciousness on this planet. This spirit exerts a powerful influence on humankind because it has existed for an unimaginably long time, ever since the creation of planet Earth, and in fact was involved in Earth's creation. Despite being the oldest spirit, the El Cantare Consciousness still works very actively, sending parts of his consciousness down to Earth to guide humankind.

The El Cantare Consciousness bears the highest responsibility for the Earth's spirit group, and it is no exaggeration to say that his character has been reflected in all the various civilizations that have bloomed on Earth. As I stated in *The Laws of the Sun*, he has lived on Earth numerous times, as La Mu of the Mu Empire, Thoth of the empire of Atlantis, Rient Arl Croud of the ancient Incan Empire, and Hermes in ancient Greece. The central task with which he is involved is creating God's Laws. This consciousness *is* God's Laws, the Laws that govern and design all of humankind. If we look at the various religions, philosophies, and ideologies that have sprung up on Earth, we find that they can all be traced back to El Cantare Consciousness. In other words, the things that he thinks about in Heaven manifest themselves on Earth in a variety of ways.

7. The Role of Jesus Christ

Jesus Christ has billions of followers, so there is little need for me to tell you about his work. But it is important to note that his spirit has been active since the creation of the Earth's spirit group, and that his principal mission is to spread love. His teachings on love reached into countries all around the world, and today, love has become a universal spiritual theme known to all people. This shows how extensively Jesus has influenced the world.

Ninth-dimensional Jesus Consciousness is also referred

to as Agasha Consciousness. Agasha was a Great Guiding Spirit of Light who appeared on Earth in Atlantis during the final period of that civilization, and Earth's spirit group is sometimes referred to as the Agasha spirit group. Agasha was the name that Jesus Consciousness took on when he incarnated in Atlantis approximately ten thousand years ago. He also appeared on Earth later, seven to eight thousand years ago, in India, where he was known as Krishna. More recently, approximately four thousand years ago, he appeared in Egypt, where he was called Clario. He never ceases to work from the ninth dimension, sending guidance to many people through many different forms.

Jesus's work is closely linked to the work of Shakyamuni. Shakyamuni's responsibilities are focused on God's Laws, which can be compared to the nervous and circulatory systems of the physical body. Like the network of veins in our bodies, they reach all parts of our being. If Shakyamuni is the brain and the creator of our arteries, veins, and capillaries, Jesus is the heart that pumps the blood throughout our body. Just as without a heart the various parts of our body would cease to function, without the work of Jesus pumping love throughout humankind, the members of the Earth's spirit group would fall into disarray, causing rampant conflict and hatred.

For hundreds of millions of years, Jesus has served as the embodiment of this mutual love, a powerful force that brings people together. And to assist him in spreading love, he has formed a large and very powerful group of healing spirits who work under his white light. Because Jesus appeared many times on Earth to spread his teachings, many spirits follow his teachings as practitioners. The seven archangels are working under Jesus's guidance as well. These spirits originally accompanied Enlil when he migrated to Earth and brought a large number of physical beings with him. But since then, they have worked principally under Jesus as his disciples.

The names of the archangels are: Michael, Gabriel, Raphael, Raguel, Sariel, Uriel, and Phanuel. (Phanuel was made an archangel to replace Lucifer after Lucifer's fall to Hell.) As leader of the archangels, Michael's role is to lead people. He has also been granted a great power to deter the workings of Satan and his followers. Gabriel is in charge of communications, and has assumed specific roles in order to contribute to various cultures and civilizations. Raphael's role is spreading love within the arts, while Sariel is leader of the spirits of healing, working to cure diseases and illnesses. In the Buddhist tradition he appears in the form of Yakushi-Nyorai (a tathagata, of medicine). He recently incarnated on Earth as Edgar Cayce. Finally, there is Uriel, who directs the field of politics.

8. The Role of Confucius

Another life force of the ninth dimension is Confucius. Born in China, he is principally the god of learning and scholarship. Scholarship is passed down from a higher level to a lower, so you can say that the Confucius Consciousness is involved with hierarchical order. Hierarchical order—the relationship between authority and obedience, dominance and submission—is one of the ways of achieving harmony, which itself is one of the two major objectives of mankind's spiritual training. Confucius has been working to create order based on the Will of God by arranging for those who are closer to God to take on authority at the upper levels of society, while those who are not as close follow them. Thus, Confucius's focus is to create an orderly society on Earth based on God's Will through the pursuit of study and the path of virtue, "the way."

To sum up the roles of these Grand Tathagatas: Shakyamuni acts as the brain that governs all systems throughout the body and as the conductor of a vast network of blood vessels throughout humankind; Jesus is the heart that pumps life-giving blood and circulates it throughout the veins; and Confucius is the coordinator who establishes order to facilitate harmony in human relationships.

If we look back over the history of humankind, we notice

that Confucius' role has contributed enormously to establishing orderly and well-regulated societies. In Heaven, some spirits have advanced to higher levels, while others are still developing in lower levels, and all of them live harmoniously in their proper places. Confucius has, indeed, played a major role in creating this orderly world.

9. The Role of Moses

Moses, who led the Israelites out of Egypt, ranks closely with Jesus and Confucius, and is primarily responsible for managing miracles. When people witness phenomena for which they have no rational or scientific explanation, they are particularly open to sensing God's hand at work. For instance, when Moses divided the Red Sea and created a path to enable the Israelites to escape the Egyptian army, or when he summoned light from Heaven to engrave the Ten Commandments in stone, people were overawed and felt the presence and power of God in these acts.

At present, Shakyamuni is actively taking the lead in establishing new cultures and civilizations, while Jesus is heading the chain of command in Heaven. Confucius is in the throes of designing plans for the evolution of humankind, and is also developing a new plan for the future of the Earth and the greater cosmos, including the roles humanity should play in the universe. Moses has been given the task of organizing the dissolution of Hell, which has been in existence now for more than one hundred million years.

EVOLUTION BEYOND
THE NINTH DIMENSION

•

What is the next level that ninth-dimensional spirits strive to move on to? When they finish their mission on planet Earth, they transfer to a new planet that is well suited to them and become leaders in their new home. They move to many different planets until they have evolved enough to become tenth-dimensional spirits.

When someone from the ninth dimension leaves Earth to live on a different planet, an eighth dimensional spirit will have a chance to move up to the ninth dimension. This is how souls evolve. This process is similar to the way people work within a company. Just as managers eventually retire, spirits on Earth who have completed their work on this planet eventually proceed to another planet. There are countless planets in the universe, and which one they choose depends on the kind of spiritual training they hope to pursue.In fact, the ten spirits of the ninth dimension on Earth are all souls who have come from other planets.

10. Revealing the World of Planetary Consciousnesses

If the ten Great Guiding Spirits carry out their work mainly in the ninth dimension, where does this light that is split into seven colors come from? It comes from the tenth dimension, the world of planetary consciousnesses. Unlike the inhabitants of the other worlds we have been describing, these spirits do not possess any of the attributes of human spirits, and have never appeared on Earth in human form.

There are three planetary consciousnesses in Earth's tenth dimension. The first is the Grand Sun Consciousness, which presides over the active principle and promotes evolution on Earth. The second is the Moon Consciousness, which governs the principles of grace and elegance, artistic beauty, abundance, and receptivity. The Grand Sun and Moon Consciousnesses combine to produce the duality of active (yang) and passive (yin) principles that make up the world as we know it. It is because of the influence of the

Moon Consciousness that the softer elements on Earth exist. Femininity stands in balance with masculinity, shade in balance with light, night in balance with day, the sea in balance with mountains, and receptivity in balance with activity.

The third member of the tenth dimension is Earth Consciousness, which has nurtured the planet and cared for all its living creatures for the last 4.6 billion years. It is the very life force of the planet itself. It creates mountains, controls volcanoes, and governs continental drift and tectonic movement. It promotes the growth of vegetation and the propagation of animals. These three consciousnesses have nurtured the planet we live on for eons and have had boundless influence on every aspect of its development.

Above the tenth dimension lies the eleventh dimension, which is where we find the stellar consciousness that governs the entire solar system. The stellar consciousness of the sun also lies in this dimension. Beyond it lies the twelfth dimension, where Galactic Consciousness resides. Finally, the thirteenth dimension provides a dwelling for the Cosmic Consciousness of the universe. This vast universe continues all the way up to the glorious Primordial God, who lies beyond the scope of our comprehension. I describe the dimensions beyond the ninth in greater detail in *The Laws of the Sun*.

As you have seen, we humans are blessed with an eternity to grow; we can continue to evolve infinitely. As we grow, we pursue a balance of evolution and harmony. This is a fundamental Truth that describes the universe that surrounds us, that encompasses all humankind. Evolution and harmony are the signposts that we should follow, and the pursuit of a balance between evolution and harmony is a process that is, at the same time, also our very goal.

In this book, *The Nine Dimensions*, I have revealed God's Truths about the world that lies beyond this one in our afterlife. I have described the structure of the spirit world from the fourth to the ninth dimensions to show you that this world that we inhabit now, the third dimension, is not the only world that exists. You have now learned that our true nature is the soul, and that our souls will continue to live in the worlds beyond, after our time on Earth is completed. It is my deepest hope that you will conduct your life based on this knowledge of God's Truths, use it to give you courage, and let it help you open a new chapter towards a more fulfilling life.

AFTERWORD

Since 1987, when this book was first published in Japanese, Happy Science has made great leaps and achieved miraculous growth. It is my conviction that the absolute Truths of the Laws I teach, and the extensiveness of these teachings, have been the forces that have propelled Happy Science through such impressive growth as a religious organization. These accomplishments prove that this is a book of God's Truths and testify that I, the deliverer of these Truths, also embody them.

The Laws in this book are *eternal*. In time, the Truths of God that I teach will be widely accepted and conveyed through time to countless generations. Those of you who have opened your spiritual eyes know that these teachings cannot be delivered through anyone but the very Creator who resides in the ninth dimension.

If Zen Buddhism is a small hill in the garden, then the enlightenment that has been put to words in this book is far taller than the majestic peaks of Mount Everest. This book is humankind's greatest hidden treasure, finally unveiled; it is El Cantare's gift of profound compassion sent to everyone living today.

Ryuho Okawa
Founder and CEO
Happy Science Group
July 1997 (Japanese Edition)

The contents of boxed text were compiled from the following sources authored by Ryuho Okawa:

1. "What Happens in the Afterlife Before Reincarnation?"

From *Hanei no Hō, Chapter 2 "Reikai no Shinsō"*
[The Laws of Prosperity, Chapter 2 "The Truth About the Spirit World"]

2. "Life in the Fifth Dimension"

From *The Science of Happiness, Chapter 3 "The Principle of the Mind"*
(Kōfuku no Genri, Chapter 3 "Kokoro no Genri")

3. "Communication in the Spirit World"

From *Hanei no Hō, Chapter 2 "Reikai no Shinsō"*
[The Laws of Prosperity, Chapter 2 "The Truth About the Spirit World"]

4. "What Are They Doing Now in Heaven? ~Einstein, Carnegie, Mozart, and Picasso~"

From *The Golden Laws, Chapter 1 "Creating a Golden Life"*
[Ōgon no Hō, Chapter 1 "Ōgon no Jinsei wo Tsukuru"]

5. "Love Incarnate"

From *The Science of Happiness, Chapter 2 "The Principle of Love"*
(Kōfuku no Genri, Chapter 2 "Ai no Genri")

6. "Evolution Beyond the Ninth Dimension"

From *Reikai Sanpo, Chapter 3 "Reikai no Fushigi (Shitsugi Ōtō)"*
[Taking a Walk in the Spirit World, Chapter 3 "The Mysteries of the Spirit World, Q & A"]

*Book titles and chapter titles in brackets have not been published in English yet, and are strictly tentative.

ABOUT THE AUTHOR

Master Ryuho Okawa started receiving messages from great historical figures—Jesus, Buddha, and others from Heaven—in 1981. These holy beings came to him with impassioned messages of urgency, entreating him to deliver their holy wisdom to people on Earth. His calling to become a spiritual leader, to inspire people all over the world with the long-hidden spiritual Truths of the origin of humankind and the soul, was revealed. These conversations unveiled the mysteries of Heaven and Hell and became the foundation on which Master Okawa built his spiritual philosophy. As his spiritual awareness deepened, he came to understand that this wisdom contained the power to help humankind overcome religious and cultural conflicts and usher in an era of peace and harmony on Earth. Just before his thirtieth birthday, Master Okawa left his promising career in business and dedicated himself to publishing the messages he receives from Heaven. Since then, he has published more than eight hundred books and become a best-selling author in Japan. The universality of the wisdom he shares, the depth of his religious and spiritual philosophy, and the clarity and compassion of his messages continue to attract hundreds of millions of readers. In addition to his ongoing writing, Master Okawa gives public talks and lectures throughout the world.

ABOUT HAPPY SCIENCE

In 1986, Master Ryuho Okawa founded Happy Science, a spiritual movement dedicated to bringing greater happiness to humankind by overcoming barriers of race, religion, and culture and by working toward the ideal of a world united in peace and harmony. Supported by followers who live in accordance with Master Okawa's words of enlightened wisdom, Happy Science has grown rapidly since its beginnings in Japan and now extends throughout the world. Today, it has more than ten million members in over eighty countries, with faith centers in New York, Los Angeles, San Francisco, Tokyo, London, Sydney, São Paulo, Seoul, and New Delhi among many other major cities. Master Okawa speaks weekly at Happy Science centers and travels around the world giving public lectures. Happy Science provides a variety of programs and services to support local communities and people in need. These programs include preschools, after-school educational programs for youths, and services for senior citizens and the disabled. Members also participate in social and charitable activities, which in the past have included providing relief aid to earthquake victims in Chile and China, raising funds for a charity school in India, and donating mosquito nets to hospitals in Uganda.

Programs and Events

Happy Science faith centers offer regular events, programs, and seminars. Join our meditation sessions, video lectures, study groups, seminars, and book events.

International Seminars

Each year, friends from all over the world join our international seminars, held at our faith centers in Japan. Different programs are offered each year and cover a wide variety of topics, including improving relationships, practicing the Eightfold Path to enlightenment, and loving yourself, to name just a few.

Happy Science Monthly

Read Master Okawa's latest lectures in our monthly booklet, *Happy Science Monthly*. You'll also find stories of members' life-changing experiences, news from Happy Science members around the world, in-depth information about Happy Science movies, book reviews, and much more. *Happy Science Monthly* is available in English, Portuguese, Spanish, French, German, Chinese, Korean, and other languages. Back issues are available upon request. Subscribe by contacting the Happy Science location nearest you.

CONTACT INFORMATION

Happy Science is a worldwide organization with faith centers around the globe. For a comprehensive list of centers, visit the worldwide directory at www.happyscience-usa.org or www.happy-science.org.

The following are a few of the many Happy Science locations:

UNITED STATES
New York
79 Franklin Street, New York, NY 10013
Phone: 212-343-7972 • Fax: 212-343-7973
Email: ny@happy-science.org
Website: www.happyscience-ny.org

Los Angeles
1590 E. Del Mar Boulevard, Pasadena, CA 91106
Phone: 626-395-7775 • Fax: 626-395-7776
Email: la@happy-science.org
Website: www.happyscience-la.org

San Francisco
525 Clinton Street, Redwood City, CA 94062
Phone/Fax: 650-363-2777
Email: sf@happy-science.org
Website: www.happyscience-sf.org

INTERNATIONAL
London
3 Margaret Street, London WIW 8RE, UK
Phone: 44-20-7323-9255 • Fax: 44-20-7323-9344
Email: eu@happy-science.org
Website: www.happyscience-eu.org

Tokyo
1-6-7 Togoshi, Shinagawa, Tokyo 142-0041 Japan
Phone: 81-3-6384-5770 • Fax: 81-3-6384-5776
Email: tokyo@happy-science.org
Website: www.kofuku-no-kagaku.or.jp/en

OTHER BOOKS BY RYUHO OKAWA

The Laws of the Sun: Discover the Origin of Your Soul

The Golden Laws: History through the Eyes of the Eternal Buddha

The Laws of Eternity: Unfolding the Secrets of the Multidimensional Universe

The Starting Point of Happiness:
A Practical and Intuitive Guide to Discovering Love, Wisdom, and Faith

Love, Nurture, and Forgive: A Handbook to Add a New Richness to Your Life

An Unshakable Mind: How to Overcome Life's Difficulties

The Origin of Love: On the Beauty of Compassion

Invincible Thinking: There is No Such Thing as Defeat

Guideposts to Happiness: Prescriptions for a Wonderful Life

The Laws of Happiness: The Four Principles for a Successful Life

Tips to Find Happiness: Creating a Harmonious Home
for Your Spouse, Your Children, and Yourself

The Philosophy of Progress:
Higher Thinking for Developing Infinite Prosperity

The Essence of Buddha: The Path to Enlightenment

The Challenge of the Mind:
A Practical Approach to the Essential Buddhist Teaching of Karma

The Challenge of Enlightenment: Realize Your Inner Potential

The Science of Happiness: 10 Principles for Manifesting Your Divine Nature

Change Your Life, Change the World: A Spiritual Guide to Living Now

The Next Great Awakening: A Spiritual Renaissance

The Moment of Truth: Become a Living Angel Today